# THE SPIRIT WITHIN YOU

### THE CHURCH'S NEGLECTED POSSESSION

*by*

## A. M. STIBBS
### and
## J. I. PACKER

SOLID GROUND CHRISTIAN BOOKS
PORT ST LUCIE, FLORIDA USA

SOLID GROUND CHRISTIAN BOOKS
1682 SW Pancoast Street
Port St Lucie FL 34987
(205) 587-4480
mike.sgcb@gmail.com
http://www.solid-ground-books.com

THE SPIRIT WITHIN YOU
*The Church's Neglected Possession*
Alan M. Stibbs
James I. Packer

First Solid Ground Edition May 2018
Published with permission of J.I. Packer

Cover Design by Borgo Design, Tuscaloosa, AL

ISBN: 978-159925-3824

**Canterbury Books** (series editor, Philip E. Hughes) are written by Anglican (Episcopalian) authors and offered as contributions of authentic Anglican thought and theology. The series will include important reprints as well as works by contemporary scholars. The significance of the subject matter, together with the quality of the writing and the reputation of the writers, is expected to ensure a wide readership for **Canterbury Books** not only among Episcopalians, but also among Christians of all denominations.

Philip Edgcumbe Hughes, Anglican scholar and author, is currently Associate Rector of St. John's Episcopal Church, Huntingdon Valley, Pennsylvania, and Visiting Professor at Westminster Theological Seminary, Philadelphia. Previously, he served in England as Vice-Principal of Tyndale Hall, Bristol; Executive Secretary of the Church Society; and Editor of *The Churchman*.

## The Story Behind This New Edition

The Lord visited me with His amazing grace in April of 1975, and within a short time I was introduced to the book *Knowing God* by J.I. Packer. That book had a profound impact on my new life in Christ and led me to begin searching for other books by the same author. Soon I found and read *Fundamentalism and the Word of God* and *Evangelism and the Sovereignty of God*. To this day over 40 years later I refer back to these books to help me keep my thoughts clear in these important areas of my walk with God.

Shortly after beginning my pastoral ministry in Amityville, Long Island, NY in the summer of 1981 I came across a copy of *The Spirit Within You* by Packer and his co-author A.M. Stibbs. It greatly ministered to me and drove me to my knees in seeking to become a faithful minister of the New Covenant. For many years I was saddened by the fact that the book was no longer available to the people of God.

Then on September 23, 2006 the hand of the Lord led me to be able to spend several hours with J.I. Packer in a church in Birmingham, Alabama. He was asked to lead a seminar entitled Theology for Everyman and as soon as I learned of it I got there early expecting a huge crowd. To my great surprise there was a very small group of people who came, and thus I was able to spend a great deal of private time with him between sessions. It was during one of those times I pulled out my dog-eared copy of *The Spirit Within You* and told him of my appreciation for the book. I then asked him if he would have any objection to me doing a new edition with Solid Ground. He said he would be delighted and gave me permission.

Nearly twelve years have come and gone, and I have finally taken up the task of bringing this out for all the world once again. Although it was over 50 years ago since the book was written, the truths set forth are as relevant today as the day these words were penned. There is still a great deal of confusion that remains concerning the person and work of the Holy Spirit, and the balanced treatment from these two dear men is as needed today as it was back then. I urge you to read this book slowly with a Bible at your side. Pray that the Spirit of the living God will open your eyes to behold the truth of The Crowning Gift of God to your eternal good.

Michael Gaydosh<br>
Solid Ground Christian Books<br>
Spring 2018

# INTRODUCTION

The authors of this essay approach their theme with the conviction that 'the gift of the Spirit to indwell God's people, corporately and individually, is the supreme and crowning blessing held forth by the Gospel'. Yet as they frankly acknowledge, the doctrine of the Spirit is tragically neglected by the Church in our day, while in some quarters strange and distorted views about the Spirit's operations are being propagated and are gaining ground.

In face of this situation they set out to examine afresh what the Bible has to say about this vitally important subject. But what they offer here is no mere academic study. They seek to relate the biblical teaching to the contemporary situation and to clarify certain issues—more especially those raised by the Pentecostal movement.

The current revival of Pentecostalism in one form or another, and its rapid spread in many parts of the world, is in part, no doubt, a rebuke to the institutionalism of the twentieth century Church. 'Where the Spirit of the Lord is', wrote the apostle, 'there is liberty'; but a rigid and narrow ecclesiastical system which tends to restrict the grace of God to episcopal channels and sacramental rites leaves little room for the Spirit to exercise His sovereign freedom or to manifest His quickening energies. The Church cannot regulate the Holy Spirit. The Church must, in fact, be regulated by the Spirit and be continually responsive to His leading, submissive to His government, loyal to His teaching.

We ignore a large area of the New Testament revelation unless we recognize that the Church is in one of its aspects the community of the Holy Spirit. It is the presence of the Spirit that constitutes the Church. And this is 'normal' Christianity, not some fanatical aberration peculiar to the sects. The gift of the Spirit is an integral part of the good news offered to men in Christ and is the common inheritance of the whole people of God. Moreover, as the authors of this essay are at pains to point out, all believers who have been 'born of the Spirit' have already received the 'baptism of the Spirit'. The Spirit's baptism is not to be regarded as a subsequent and additional endowment, enjoyed by a select minority and manifested in such spectacular gifts as speaking in tongues. This, they insist, is a misreading of the New Testament evidence and can only give rise to spiritual confusion and frustration.

It is our hope, as it is theirs, that what they have written may help towards a recovery in the Church today not only of a truer doctrine of the Spirit but also of a deepening apprehension and experience of the pentecostal gift—the Church's neglected possession.

PHILIP E. HUGHES<br>
FRANK COLQUHOUN<br>
Joint Editors

# CONTENTS

| | Page |
|---|---|
| Introduction | 5 |
| 1 GOD'S CROWNING GIFT | 9 |
| 2 WIDESPREAD MISUNDERSTANDING | 15 |
| 3 GOVERNING SANCTIONS | 21 |
| 4 THE PENTECOSTAL GIFT | 27 |
| 5 RECEIVING THE SPIRIT | 37 |
| 6 WALKING BY THE SPIRIT | 46 |
| 7 THE FULNESS OF THE SPIRIT | 58 |
| 8 THE FELLOWSHIP OF THE CHURCH | 68 |
| 9 THE LEADING OF THE SPIRIT | 77 |
| 10 ASSURANCE AND HOPE | 85 |

*Note:* Biblical quotations unless otherwise stated are taken from the American Revised Standard Version of the Bible.

# ACKNOWLEDGMENTS

The authors would like to thank the following for giving them their permission to quote:

Oxford University Press and Cambridge University Press for quotations from the *New English Bible*.

Thomas Nelson and Sons Ltd. for quotations from the *Revised Standard Version of the Bible*.

CHAPTER ONE

# GOD'S CROWNING GIFT

'No, we have never even heard that there is a Holy Spirit.' Such was the reply of the Ephesian disciples to St. Paul's question, 'Did you receive the Holy Spirit when you believed?' (Acts 19: 2). Their words express a state of mind to which the modern Church, to put it mildly, is no stranger. The Holy Spirit has justly been described as 'the displaced person of the Godhead.' The presence in some quarters of strange and distorted views about the Spirit's operations is regrettable, no doubt, but much more regrettable is the widespread absence of truer teaching.

Imagine an enquirer attending an ordinary parish church, or visiting a whole number of them for that matter, for an entire year. Would he by the end of that time, do you think, have become fully convinced that the gift of the Spirit to indwell God's people, corporately and individually, is the supreme and crowning blessing held forth by the Gospel? It is doubtful, isn't it? He might well have learned much about the place and work of Jesus Christ, the way of repentance and forgiveness, the needs of the Church, and the tasks of Christians; but would he, even in these contexts, have heard very much about the Holy Spirit? We need frankly to recognize that explicit teaching concerning the Holy Spirit, leading Christians to appreciate the real significance of His indwelling and to experience the fulness of His power, is a sadly rare thing at the present time.

Yet the Bible sets forth the bestowal and ministry of the Spirit as the true climax of God's generosity, and the supreme glory of this gospel age. In the circumstances, we had better begin our present study by showing this in some detail.

## THE SPIRIT POURED OUT

At Jacob's well, speaking to a Samaritan woman, Jesus said: 'If you knew *the gift of God*, and who it is that is saying to you, "Give me a drink," you would have asked him, and he would have given you living water.' 'Whoever drinks,' He added, 'of the water that I shall give him will never thirst; the water that I shall give him will become in him a spring of water welling up to eternal life' (Jn. 4: 10, 14). What was 'the gift of God', the thirst-quenching water to be received from the hand of Jesus? St. John's comment on Jesus' later reference to 'rivers of living water' flowing out of the believer's inmost being surely makes this plain: 'This he said about the Spirit, which those who believed in him were to receive' (Jn. 7: 38f.). 'The gift of God', *the* gift *par excellence*, is the Holy Spirit.

Again, after His resurrection Jesus charged His disciples 'not to depart from Jerusalem, but to wait for *the promise of the Father*, which, he said, "you heard from me, for John baptized with water, but before many days you shall be baptized with the Holy Spirit" (Acts 1: 4f.). Here, too, Jesus was speaking—and this time explicitly—of God's gift of the Holy Spirit.

The experience and enjoyment of the personal presence of God the Spirit is set forth as the distinctive feature of God's New Covenant, and of the so-called last days; that is, the days of the consummation and realized fulfilment of God's purposes towards men in Christ. 'This is what was spoken by the prophet Joel: "And in the last days it shall be, God declares, that *I will pour out my Spirit* upon all flesh"' (Acts 2: 16f.; citing Joel 2: 28). This is how, on the day of Pentecost, St. Peter began his explanation of what had happened in the upper room. The Spirit had been poured out; a new era had begun.

So, in contrast to God's giving of the Law at Sinai, which was in relation to sinful men a dispensation of condemnation and death, the New Covenant is described by St. Paul as 'the dispensation of the Spirit'. Its power to make men live as they should lies 'not in a written code but in the Spirit; for the written code kills, but the Spirit gives life' (see II Cor. 3: 5–9). The Holy Spirit, given through the Gospel, makes possible for us holy and victorious living, springing from the experience of divine grace into which He leads us. It is in the character of the Christian Gospel as 'the dispensation of the Spirit' that its supreme glory lies.

## THE GIFT OURS BY GOD'S WILL AND CHRIST'S WORK

God's gift of the Spirit to men through the Gospel is His fulfilment of the promise to Abraham that in him and in his seed all the nations of the earth should be blessed. (See Gen. 12: 3; 22: 18.) St. Paul wrote: 'Christ redeemed us from the curse of the law . . . that in Christ Jesus *the blessing of Abraham* might come upon the Gentiles, that *we might receive the promise of the Spirit through faith*' (Gal. 3: 13f.).

The Spirit's coming to indwell men is therefore dependent upon both the will of God the Father and the work of God the Son, In His earthly life, death and resurrection, Jesus acted in obedience in order to fulfil His Father's foreordained purpose, and so to make possible the gift to men of God the Spirit. Without the redeeming and saving work of Christ for us, the regenerating and sanctifying work of the Spirit in us would be impossible. In the language of Old Testament figure, only after the rock was smitten did the waters flow. The Spirit was not given until, His earthly work finished, Jesus had been glorified. (See Jn. 7: 39.)

The Spirit's incoming to indwell God's people completes the work of the whole Trinity for man's redemption. St. Paul briefly summarizes the full truth when he says: 'But when the time had fully come, God sent forth his Son, born of woman, born under the law, to redeem those who were under the law, so that we might receive adoption as sons. And because you are sons, God has sent the Spirit of his Son into our hearts, crying, "Abba! Father!"' (Gal. 4: 4–6). The incoming of the Spirit into our hearts, there to abide, is the climax and completion of the activity for our benefit of the whole Godhead, Father, Son, and Spirit.

### THE GIFT GIVEN TO ALL WHO BELIEVE

Consequently the New Testament repeatedly emphasizes that once individuals believe in Christ, once they are baptized in His name, and become Christians, then this gift of the Spirit is already theirs. They do not now have to seek it as a second, subsequent blessing, complementary to conversion. For this gift is itself the initial and initiating gift of God, by which in the moment of their salvation and regeneration men are baptized into the one body of Christ. So, on the day of Pentecost, Peter said to convicted enquirers, 'Repent, and be baptized every one of you in the name of Jesus Christ for the forgiveness of your sins; *and you shall receive the gift of the Holy Spirit.* For the promise is to you and to your children and to all that are far off, *every one* whom the Lord our God calls to him' (Acts 2: 38f.).

Statements in the epistles enforce the truth that all believers have the Spirit indwelling them. In Romans 5 Paul outlines the far-reaching consequences of our being 'justified by faith'. Among these he refers to 'the Holy Spirit *which has been given to us*' (Rom. 5: 5). Again, in Romans 8: 9–11 Paul encourages his readers to realize the blessings that are theirs to enjoy—life and peace here (cf. v. 6), and a glorious resurrection hereafter—in virtue of the fact that 'the Spirit of God *really dwells in you*'. (The 'if' which introduces these words, like that which opens verses 10 and 11, expresses not a doubt but a presupposition, which provides the ground for the statements which follow. A similar usage occurs in I Thess. 4: 14 and I Pet. 2: 3. That Paul is sure that his readers, as Christians, are indwelt by the Spirit appears from his comment in the second half of verse 9: 'Any one who does not have the Spirit of Christ does not belong to him'; that is, he is not a true Christian at all.)

Again, when Paul tells the Thessalonian Christians that 'God has not called us for uncleanness but in holiness', he adds:

'Therefore whoever disregards this, disregards not man but God, who gives his Holy Spirit to you' (I Thess. 4: 7f.). Paul means that God has made holy living possible for all Christians by His gift of His indwelling Spirit. Christians do not have to wait for the Spirit, but to 'walk by the Spirit' who indwells them already, and so rise above the desires of the flesh. (See Gal. 5: 16.)

Writing to the Corinthians Paul says, 'Do you not know that your body is a temple of the Holy Spirit within you, *which you have from God?*' (I Cor. 6: 19). Later, in his second letter to them, and with reference to our God-given hope of a 'heavenly dwelling' or resurrection body, Paul declares, 'He who has prepared us for this very thing is God, *who has given us the Spirit* as a guarantee' (II Cor. 5: 5). Paul's teaching is clear. All Christians have the God-given Spirit dwelling within them.

Nor does St. John speak differently. Rather he appeals to the witness of the God-given Spirit as evidence of our personal communion with God. 'By this we know', he writes, 'that he abides in us, by *the Spirit which he has given us*' (I Jn. 3: 24). This truth is, indeed, so important that he repeats it. 'By this we know that we abide in him and he in us, because *he has given us of his own Spirit*' (I Jn. 4: 13).

Surely these statements speak for themselves and confirm one another. Their message is unmistakably plain. All true Christians have received God's gift of His indwelling Spirit. Those, therefore, who suppose that the Spirit may not be given to a man till some time after he becomes a Christian are mistaken. Some have suggested, for instance, that believers receive 'the seal of the Spirit' (see Eph. 1: 13; 4: 30; II Cor. 1: 22) only at confirmation by a bishop; others, that a 'second act of faith', with a corresponding 'second blessing', is required before Christians 'possess' the Spirit (as if the question were not rather, whether, or how far, *He* possesses *us!*). Others, again, have taught that a Christian does not have the Spirit in any significant sense till he has received a conscious 'baptism in the Spirit', marked (it has frequently been said) by speaking in tongues. But the New Testament takes a different line from all these. It starts by insisting that under the new covenant the Holy Spirit indwells all believers, as such, from the moment of their believing, however little they may be aware of it. Then it proceeds, on that basis, to summon us to the holy living which has now become possible for us, and to lead us into the assurance and joy which the Spirit's indwelling both warrants and begets. To explore these themes is our present purpose.

CHAPTER TWO

# WIDESPREAD MISUNDERSTANDING

As we have just said, in this realm of the reception and enjoyment of God's gift in Christ of the indwelling Spirit there is widespread misunderstanding, not merely by uninformed outsiders, but among many true believers in Christ. In this chapter we seek to expose in more detail the varied forms of such misunderstanding, not in any censorious spirit, but simply to promote fresh personal self-examination. Only those who are willing to learn where they are mistaken or come short, can hope to enter into the liberating light of divinely-revealed truth. The writers' hope is that those who read will, before going further, prepare themselves to be readers of this sort.

### GOD'S INITIAL GIFT UNAPPRECIATED

Misunderstanding by individual Christians often begins at the point of their entrance into the experience of personal salvation through faith in Christ crucified and risen. This happens because the Gospel which they embrace, and in which they rightly begin to glory, is incompletely understood. Perhaps it has been incompletely presented. Do preachers always stress, as they should, the gift of the Spirit as part of the good news? (See Acts 2: 38f.) In any case it is easy for young Christians to miss the significance of this part of the message. They are made convincingly aware that through Christ's death and resurrection their sins are forgiven and blotted out, and they themselves are justified—that is, accepted as righteous—in God's sight. These benefits are so wonderful, and so rich a source of joy, that new believers can hardly at first spare a thought for anything else. But the benefits do not end here; there is more to God's salvation even than this; and those who turn from sin to trust in Christ for salvation ought equally to be made aware that the exalted Jesus, whom they now confess as Lord, has also exercised towards them His unique prerogative as God's Christ, and baptized them with the Holy Spirit. They should be taught from the first that by this baptism they were both regenerated—that is, given new life—and also incorporated into the one Church, the body of Christ—that is, into the community of the redeemed who are born again of God's Spirit. 'By one Spirit we were all baptized into one body,' wrote St. Paul to the Corinthian Christians (I Cor. 12: 13). The 'body' is Christ's Church, and the baptizer is Christ Himself.

### A FURTHER 'BAPTISM' MISTAKENLY SOUGHT

If this further element of the Gospel of salvation in Christ is not fully grasped, serious consequences may ensue. In the first place, the justification thus enjoyed in God's sight may appear to be—some, indeed, caricature it as—a mere pretence, a legal fiction, making no vital and practical difference to the person on whom it is conferred. The full truth, however, is that once a sinner is thus put right with God he is immediately given the life-giving Spirit. He is then and there born again; and he ought to know that the Spirit of God now dwells in him.

But, as we said, many who have found peace with God in Christ do not at first appreciate this. Then, being eager as Christians for God's best, and having discovered from God's Word that only by the Spirit can a holy and fruitful life be lived, the danger is that they will begin to think, or will be readily persuaded by others, that they must now seek from God a second complementary blessing, a further 'gift of the Spirit', as something distinct from the salvation they have enjoyed so far. So they set themselves to seek what they already have, often using the term 'baptism' to describe this further endowment—to be given, as they think, subsequent to their justification by faith. Scripturally, however, as we saw, the phrase 'baptism in (with, by) the Spirit' should be applied only to the initial and initiating endowment of the indwelling Spirit which Christ as Lord gives to all whom He makes, and marks as, His own.

### CHURCH MEMBERSHIP NEGLECTED

In the second place, failure to appreciate the real character and consequence of the true baptism in the Spirit results in a grievous neglect of church membership. The New Testament teaches that 'by one Spirit we were all baptized into one body ... and all were made to drink of one Spirit' (I Cor. 12: 13). This means that not only is the gift of the Spirit given equally to all alike, but also that one great positive effect of this baptism is to incorporate us into the one body of Christ, a living organism in which we are all meant to function together as living members. The baptism of the Spirit rightly understood is, therefore, an equipment for, and a call to, active church membership.

In radical contrast to this, individual Christians who seek, or claim to have experienced, the baptism of the Spirit as a second subsequent blessing commonly—and wrongly—think of it as an individual experience, intended, it may be, for the whole Church, but actually entered into only by a privileged few, who constitute thenceforth a kind of spiritual élite, and whose relation to the rest of the visible Church, who lack this experience, may lawfully become somewhat loose. But this is the opposite of the New Testament idea of Spirit-baptism, which is of an initiating event common to all Christians, bringing them from the start into the full community life as functioning church members.

### THE GIFT INSTITUTIONALIZED

In contrast to those who sit loose to the God-given privileges and obligations of church membership, others are over-conscious of 'the Church' as an institution, and wish to give it a place and function which the Gospel and the New Testament do not give it, in conferring the Spirit upon individual Christians.

What the New Testament teaches is that to baptize with the Spirit is the unique prerogative of God's Christ. All therefore who would enjoy this blessing must look direct to Christ in faith, and call upon His name as Lord. For while ministers of the Church may, like John the Baptist, baptize with water, only Christ can baptize with the Holy Spirit. By this baptism He quickens those dead in sin into new life, and at the same time initiates them into vital membership in the saved community. The Lord Himself thus adds to the Church those who are being saved (Acts 2: 47).

Some appear to hold that individuals receive the Spirit, and so are joined to Christ as Lord, by dependence upon the visible Church, and by initiation into it, or sustained communion with it, through its proper ministers. The full giving of the Spirit to men, and the experience by individuals of the benefits of His incoming, are thus in effect tied up either to episcopal activity in confirmation and ordination, or to the administration of the sacraments by a properly ordained priest. This is the recurring blight of ecclesiastical formalism, the occupational risk of those who hold—as Christians must—a strong doctrine of the Church. Corruption of the best produces the worst.

### THE GIFT AND THE GIVER SUPERSEDED

At its worst, this tendency of thought and practice offers men the supposed benefits of ecclesiastical ceremonies as substitutes for the true Gift and the true Giver. So, for instance, in some circles men are said at the time of their death to have been 'fortified by the rites of the Church', when true Christian faith would desire to see them fortified by Christ through the Spirit. Christ and the Spirit are thus eclipsed or obscured in men's thought and faith by the Church and her ceremonies. Some types of so-called 'catholic' theology seem to have no proper doctrine of the Holy Spirit; a doctrine of the sacraments is preferred instead. To take a random example: in *The Christian Sacraments* by O. C. Quick, a work of some 250 pages, the person and work of the Holy Spirit are scarcely mentioned, and this is not an isolated case. At its worst, indeed, the whole Trinity is obscured by this kind of teaching. Instead of men being offered life from God in Christ and by the Spirit they are encouraged to expect help from the Church through the priest and by the sacrament. The gravity of this misrepresentation seems rarely to be recognized, though in principle it appears comparable to the sin of Jeroboam the son of Nebat, who made Israel to sin (see I Ki. 12: 25-30).

### MISPLACED PASSIVITY

At the other extreme are Christians who are so persuaded that God is sovereign in quickening man by the Spirit, that they think it right always to wait for God to stir them to action by direct inward prompting, believing that any initiative on their part would be a lapse into carnal self-reliance. But the truth plainly reiterated in the epistles of the New Testament is that, because the Spirit is given to us, new action on our part is now possible. God Himself calls us to rise from our inactivity and to 'walk by the Spirit'. Not until we do so act will the full outworked benefits of the indwelling Spirit become ours in realized experience. Complete passivity here, however pious and well-intentioned, is disastrously misplaced.

### DANGEROUS PRESUMPTION

Again, there are those who, just because they are so sure that the God-given Spirit does indwell and guide the Church, are prone to assume that any apparently attractive new movement among Christians should be attributed to the Spirit's activity, and therefore be welcomed and supported. So, for instance, many would assume that any step which appears to bring closer Christians who are outwardly separated is Spirit-prompted, no matter what it may involve in terms of sacrifice of principle or disregard of deep-seated conscientious misgiving. Such enthusiasts for action put to shame many who do nothing; yet they show a potentially fatal weakness, in that they lack any adequate governing sanctions by which to distinguish the leading of the Spirit from influences not of His originating. For it is not the Spirit of God who encourages disregard of conscience and unconcern for truth. A speaker at an ecumenical gathering once opposed a statement which affirmed that it would be wrong to sacrifice principles in the interests of practical advance by saying: 'Surely there is nothing else that is worth sacrificing!' But this shocking remark does not express the mind of the Holy Spirit.

### DEFICIENT OBEDIENCE

Finally, we must note the inconsistency of those who will not follow out the implications of objective evidence which is unmistakably Spirit-given, when it conflicts with their personal prejudices and traditional preferences. When Barnabas was sent by the Church in Jerusalem to the unconventional new church at Antioch, he was rightly glad to enter into full fellowship in Christ with them, because he saw the grace of God active among them (Acts 11: 22–26). In the same way those reputed to be pillars of the Church in Jerusalem rightly gave to Paul and Barnabas the right hand of fellowship as fellow-ministers of the Gospel when they saw that the Spirit of God was savingly active through their ministry (see Gal. 2: 6–9). Yet in our day (and, sad to confess, in our Anglican communion) there are those who have acknowledged the unmistakable grace of God in the Free Churches and their ministries, and yet decline to join with them in full Christian fellowship at the Lord's Table as brethren in Christ; nor will they give to their ministers the right hand of fellowship as equal partners in the work of the Gospel. This deplorable reluctance, however motivated, flies in the face of reality and truth, and cannot but grieve the Holy Spirit.

CHAPTER THREE

## GOVERNING SANCTIONS

In considering the nature and intended consequences of God's crowning gift of His Spirit to indwell His people, two complementary truths must be recognized. On the one hand this gift ensures, by God's own activity within us, the full realization of His purposes for us, a fulfilment impossible except in this way. On the other hand this is a sphere in which it is all too possible for individuals to be deceived and misled. We must therefore be on our guard, and seek to be ready to exercise necessary discernment and discrimination. As we have just seen, not every idea or practice which appears to be 'spiritual' is inspired by the Holy Spirit of God.

### THE POSSIBILITY OF DECEPTION

There are in the New Testament explicit warnings of the danger of being misled. In I Corinthians, when Paul introduces the subject of spiritual gifts he begins by alerting his readers to this peril by reminding them of their own pre-Christian experience. 'You know how', he writes, 'in the days when you were still pagan, you were swept off to those dumb heathen gods, however you happened to be led' (I Cor. 12: 2, N.E.B.). Later, in his second letter to the Corinthians, he bluntly exposes some as 'false apostles, deceitful workmen, disguising themselves as apostles of Christ', and he adds, 'There is nothing surprising about that; Satan himself masquerades as an angel of light' (II Cor. 11: 13f. R.S.V. and N.E.B.). Similarly St. John wrote: 'But do not trust any and every spirit, my friends; test the spirits, to see whether they are from God, for among those who have gone out into the world there are many prophets falsely inspired' (I Jn. 4: 1, N.E.B.).

So, in the interests of our own spiritual safety and well-being, we need to know how the indwelling Spirit may be expected to function; what are the divinely-intended purposes and ends for which He is thus given to indwell us; and, in particular, what are the sanctions and tests by which we may make sure that it is His activity that we are experiencing.

### TWO DEFINITIVE ACTIVITIES OF THE SPIRIT

Our thinking about these questions should start from the fact that the Spirit is the agent of special activities of God towards sinful men in both revelation and redemption. In the first place, the Spirit is especially connected with illumination and insight, with prophecy and utterance, and so with the inspiration of the Scriptures of both the Old and the New Testaments. This revelation is primarily of Christ, and of God's purposes for men in and through Him. The Old Testament Scriptures 'bear witness to me', declared Jesus (Jn. 5: 39). 'The testimony of Jesus is the spirit of prophecy', wrote the seer (Rev. 19: 10). St. Peter tells us that 'the Spirit of Christ' inspired the testimony to Jesus borne by Old Testament prophets, just as He empowered the New Testament preachers of the Gospel (I Pet. 1: 10–12). Jesus described the specific new covenant ministry which the Spirit would fulfil in the words: 'he will bear witness of me'; 'he will glorify me' (Jn. 15: 26; 16: 14).

In the second place, the final activity of God in sending His Son to save men was similarly effected through the Spirit. When the eternal Son of God became Man, His conception, anointing, ministry, offering of Himself, and His resurrection are all said to have been done through and by the Spirit. (See Mt. 1: 20; Lk. 1: 35; 3: 21f.; Jn. 1: 33; Lk. 4: 18, with Acts 10: 38; Lk. 4: 14; Mt. 12: 28; Rom. 8: 11; Heb. 9: 14; I Pet. 3: 18.)

### TWO CONSEQUENT DETERMINING SANCTIONS

These two 'once for all' activities of the Spirit in human history, in the production of both the written and the incarnate Word of revelation and redemption, provide two decisive and abiding tests of the Spirit's identity. For He does not contradict Himself or go back on His mission among men. Therefore, any present witness or activity which is truly His will both be in harmony with the written Word, and also confess Jesus as God manifest in the flesh.

These two sanctions are explicitly enunciated and applied in the Scriptures. In the days of Isaiah, when some claimed through mediums and wizards to have messages from God, the test to be applied was this: 'To the law and to the testimony! if they speak not *according to this word*, surely there is no morning for them', or 'light in them' (Is. 8: 20, R.V. and A.V.). Similarly, when in the early Church Christians were being misled by false prophets, John wrote: 'By this you know the Spirit of God: every spirit which *confesses that Jesus Christ has come in the flesh* is of God, and every Spirit which does not confess Jesus is not of God' (I Jn. 4: 2f.). And in the same connection Paul wrote, 'Therefore I want you to understand that no one speaking by the Spirit of God ever says "Jesus be cursed!" and *no one can say "Jesus is Lord" except by the Holy Spirit*' (I Cor. 12: 3).

Both tests must still be applied, if we are to be preserved from being misled by persons who may unjustifiably claim, and even attractively appear to have, the leading of the Spirit. We must still ask, Is what they say or do supported by, and not contrary to, the witness of the Bible? And do they fully and sincerely acknowledge Jesus, crucified and risen, as God incarnate?

### TWO CORRESPONDING SPIRITUAL BENEFITS

Nor do the confirming sanctions end there. Complementary evidence may be expected in the experience of those who accept the scriptural testimony and confess Jesus as divine Saviour and Lord. For it is the continuing work of the Spirit of revelation to produce in those of whom He takes possession deep conviction of sin (cf. Jn. 16: 8); to inspire personal confession of Christ (cf. Acts 4: 31); to give growing understanding in and through the study of the written Word (cf. I Jn. 2: 20, 27); and to produce strong assurance of peace with God, acceptance in God's sight, access to His presence, and the hope of His glory (cf. Eph. 1: 17–19). By these practical tests we may examine ourselves to see whether the Spirit of revelation is truly operative in our experience, increasing and deepening our knowledge of God.

It is also the present work of the Spirit, whom Christ as Saviour gives to His people, to work out in them the results of what Christ has wrought for them, and to make the enjoyment of salvation and progress in sanctification a practical reality in their experience. As the Spirit of Christ, it is His special task to induce increasingly in those whom He indwells the 'fruit' of Christlike character (Gal. 5: 22f.; II Cor. 3: 18). All God's children must bear the family likeness (cf. Rom. 8: 29); all whose bodies are temples of the Holy Spirit must be holy in their conduct (cf. I Cor. 6: 19f.). The way of life is 'by the Spirit' to 'put to death the deeds of the body'; this, before anything else, is what it means to be 'led by the Spirit of God' (Rom. 8: 13f.). Again, it is through examining ourselves by these practical standards that we may discover how far we are actually experiencing the divinely-intended consequences of God's gift to us in Christ of His indwelling Spirit.

Such properly informed self-examination is the more necessary because it is all too easy to covet temporary and possibly sensational 'manifestations' of the Spirit without any proper interest in those which are permanent and morally substantial. There seems special need to warn against this pitfall at the present time.

THE PRE-EMINENCE OF CHRIST AS LORD

In and through all this activity the Spirit's primary concern is to glorify Christ, to secure the acknowledgment and the practical outworking of His lordship in the lives of men. It is clear that Christ can be thus properly known and worthily served only by the aid of the combined ministries of the revealing Word and the enlightening Spirit. But, while the ministries of the written Word and the indwelling Spirit are therefore indispensable, we must never become occupied with them as ends in themselves. Their single dominant purpose lies beyond themselves, in the doing of God's will and in the exaltation of His Christ. Here, then, is the supreme and final test of the genuineness of any professed experience of the Spirit's activity. Is it part of this experience that the Spirit, by the constant use of God's written Word, promotes in our daily lives the realized lordship of Christ and the actual doing of God's will?

### OTHER COMPLEMENTARY TESTS

The fulfilment of such an all-embracing objective will necessarily draw forth from us a variety of contributing characteristics, all of which should—at least in some measure—be present and constantly on the increase in our lives. If the indwelling Spirit is active and unquenched within us, then there will be manifest, as we saw, the fruit of the Spirit in Christ-like character and conduct. There will be evangelistic and missionary zeal to make the Gospel of Christ known both to our neighbours and to the ends of the earth. There will be realized fellowship in Christ with fellow-believers. There will be liberty together in prayer and worship. There will be an active and practical love of the brethren. There should be an exercise of varied ministries, which are edifying to one and all. There will be a steadfast continuance in discipleship and devotion, particularly when facing trial or persecution; and we shall find in ourselves a readiness to be faithful unto death.

When we measure ourselves by these standards, we are made painfully aware how far short we all fall of the divine intention. Who knows as much of the Spirit's ministry as he should? Who dare imagine for one moment that he has no need to learn, and experience, more? Let us then, through the chapters which follow, seek to grasp with fresh clarity how the blessing and the benefits of the indwelling Spirit are meant to become ours both in our individual and in our corporate experience. All that has been said so far has been general and introductory; now we get down to a more exact treatment of this great and vital theme.

CHAPTER FOUR

# THE PENTECOSTAL GIFT

In our first chapter we laid it down that the indwelling Spirit is God's crowning gift under the New Covenant, and that all believers, right from the start of their Christian lives, are possessors of this gift. In affirming the second of these two positions, however, we begged several important and much-discussed questions, and it is necessary now to go back and face some of these squarely.

## THE NEW COVENANT GIFT

First, we must ask, In what is the new covenant gift of the Spirit distinctive? How does the Spirit's post-Pentecostal ministry differ from its pre-Pentecostal counterpart? Undoubtedly, both revelation and regeneration took place in many human lives from Adam's time down to Christ's. Abel, Abraham, all the godly in Israel, and many who came to faith under the preaching of our Lord Himself—among whom eleven of the twelve disciples must be included (see Jn. 13: 10f.; 15: 3; 17: 6-19)—were subjects of the Spirit's ministry prior to Pentecost. What difference then did Pentecost make? What was the new thing that began then? John the Baptist served God before Pentecost, Stephen after; both were men 'filled with the Holy Spirit' (Lk. 1: 15; Acts 6: 5; 7: 55); was there any decisive difference between them? When the Spirit fell on men at and after Pentecost, they spoke with tongues, prophesied, healed, and wrought miracles; was this the essence of the decisive new thing that Pentecost brought? If so, why does the Church no longer exercise, nor (so it seems) value, these particular ministries? If not, what was the distinctive work of the Spirit that began at Pentecost, and where did the special manifestations fit in?

To answer one of these questions, we offer the following line of thought. The rector of a well-known church in London was previously its assistant curate. The question, 'When did the rector *come* to this church?' cannot therefore be answered without making a distinction. One has to say that he came as curate in 1945, and began his work as rector in 1950. From one standpoint, his ministry was continuous and homogeneous, for he did not abandon in 1950 any of the activities which he had been performing during the previous five years, nor did his ministry after 1950 take on any noticeably different outward character. He has done little since 1950 which he did not from time to time, in some shape or form, do before. From another standpoint, however, 1950 marked a new departure; the new responsibilities which he assumed in that year were such that he could truly be said to be starting a new job.

Something similar must be said of the Holy Spirit. Prior to Pentecost He had been active in Israel, mediating knowledge, faith, sanctification, and fellowship with God, and this He has not ceased to do. But at Pentecost He began to perform a new task—one which imparted a fresh quality or dimension to each aspect of His ministry to individuals, so that the whole of it, viewed from one standpoint, has taken on a new and enhanced character.

This change corresponds to, and indeed depends on, what was equally true concerning men's enjoyment of the benefits of Christ's atoning sacrifice. In Old Testament times the benefits of Christ's death were experienced by faith before Christ's actual crucifixion. It was, as Paul expresses it (see Rom. 3: 25), Christ's propitiatory sacrifice that justified the divine forbearance in passing over sins committed before Christ came. But the way in which men then enjoyed these benefits was limited to the Jewish people, by incomplete fulfilment, and by necessary ceremonial anticipation. Only when the fulness of time came and the one all-sufficient sacrifice for sins was offered once for all was the gospel of salvation fully revealed, and its proclamation extended to all men everywhere.

Similarly the full activity of the Spirit under the New

Covenant was one which in the nature of the case He could not begin till Jesus, having made atonement for our sins, was risen and ascended. For this new task was precisely to glorify before men's eyes the glorified Jesus of Nazareth—that is, to make them see the glory of His finished work of redemption, to make His presence with them, as the reigning Lord, a conscious reality, to unite them to Him in His risen life and make them understand what this union means, and to lead them into the wealth of the salvation which He had won for them.

This was the distinctive new covenant ministry which the Spirit began on a permanent basis during the morning of the day of Pentecost following Jesus' ascension. Thus it is now the Spirit's work, first, to convince sinners of the truth concerning Jesus the Saviour and to lead them to faith in Him; and then to make theirs in experience all the benefits now available to be enjoyed in consequence of Christ's saving work. He does this by taking up His residence in the hearts of all believers in Christ in order constantly to fulfil this ministry towards them. (See Jn. 14: 16-23; 15: 26f.; 16: 7-15.) Once we grasp this, various things become clear. We see why, when reporting Jesus' promise that 'rivers of living water' should flow from believers' hearts, John commented: 'this he said about the Spirit, which those who believed in Him were to receive; *for as yet the Spirit had not been given, because Jesus was not yet glorified*' (Jn. 7: 39). It is the special new covenant activity of the Spirit, as He glorifies the glorified Christ in men's eyes as their Saviour, which gives Christian experience its characteristic quality. This ministry could not start till Jesus, having put away the sin of the world, was triumphantly enthroned in heaven. The 'giving' and 'receiving' of the Spirit to fulfil this ministry had to wait, therefore, till after the ascension.

But once His atoning and reconciling work was done, the risen Lord solemnly assured His disciples that His donation and their reception of the Spirit would now take place. So, we read, 'He breathed on them, and said to them, "Receive the Holy Spirit" ' (Jn. 20: 22). This does not imply that the actual gift was then and there made; otherwise the events of the day of Pentecost would lose their meaning. What Jesus hereby gave the disciples was an acted sign and pledge that the gift was now as good as theirs. He complemented this by telling them before His ascension, 'Behold, I send the promise of my Father upon you; but stay in the city, until you are clothed with power from on high' (Lk. 24: 49).

This promise the ascended Jesus duly fulfilled on the day of Pentecost. In explanation of the disciples' transforming experience on that day Peter declared concerning 'this Jesus' that 'being therefore exalted at the right hand of God, and having received from the Father the promise of the Holy Spirit, he has poured out this which you see and hear' (Acts 2: 33). Peter went on to tell his hearers that, if they would repent and be baptized in the name of Jesus Christ for the forgiveness of sins, they too would receive the gift of the Holy Spirit. 'For,' he said, 'the promise is to you and to your children and to all that are far off, every one whom the Lord Our God calls to him' (Acts 2: 38f.). So the new covenant ministry of the Spirit, achieved by His coming to dwell permanently within every believer in Christ, is now offered, to begin at once, to all who heed the call of God in the gospel, and turn to Christ in repentance and faith.

### THE SPECIAL MANIFESTATIONS

What, then, was the significance of the special manifestations of the Spirit's presence,—speaking in tongues, prophesying, healing, working miracles, and so forth—which began at, and continued after, the pentecostal outpouring, both in the experience of the apostles themselves, and in the lives of Christians and churches to whom they ministered? The fascinating problems which arise regarding the exact nature of these manifestations must here be passed by; suffice it to say simply that the primary purpose of them was to *authenticate* the apostles as true messengers, their Gospel as a true message, and their converts as true members of the new covenant fellowship. Just as the Lord's healings were signs of His messiahship (see Mt. 11: 2–6), so these supernatural manifestations granted in connection with the apostles' ministry were signs of the present reality of the realm of grace and spiritual renewal which Jesus had called 'the kingdom of God', the realm of which the apostles were heralds, their Gospel was the charter, and all believers became citizens.

Various Scriptures show this. In his pentecostal sermon, Peter appealed to 'this which you see and hear' as evidence of Jesus' resurrection and reign (Acts 2: 33). The writer to the Hebrews speaks of the 'great salvation' preached by Jesus and 'attested to us by those who heard him, while *God also bore witness* by signs and wonders and by various miracles and by gifts of the Holy Spirit distributed according to his own will' (Heb. 2: 3f.). St. Paul referred to 'signs and wonders and mighty works' wrought by him among the Corinthians, and called them 'the signs of a true apostle' (II Cor. 12: 12). Reporting at Jerusalem the conversion of Cornelius and his family, St. Peter explained, and his hearers could not but agree, that the immediately discernible signs of the outpouring of the Spirit upon these Gentiles was clear evidence that God had effectively brought them into the reality of Christian salvation, so that it was right to admit them formally into the Church by baptism and treat them henceforth as brethren. "As I began to speak, the Holy Spirit fell on them just as on us at the beginning ... If then God gave the same gift to them as He gave to us when we believed in the Lord Jesus Christ, who was I that I could withstand God?" When they heard this they [those who had at first censured Peter for fraternizing with Gentiles] were silenced. And they glorified God, saying, "Then to the Gentiles also God has granted repentance unto life" ' (Acts 11: 15–18).

Talk of a revival of similar manifestations of the Spirit's presence is common today in some circles. But we should weigh the following facts. (1) So far as we can judge from the New Testament, these manifestations were always given in connection with the apostles' personal ministry. Certainly, they died out rapidly at the end of the apostolic age. (2) The New

Testament contains no specific promise either of their continuance or of their renewal in any post-pentecostal situation. (Mark 16: 17f., as is well known, was no part of St. Mark's original text.) (3) Nowhere in the New Testament are such manifestations regarded as indispensable for the health of the Church. In I Corinthians 12–14, Paul insists that in the congregation spiritual gifts must be used in an edifying, and not an unedifying, fashion; and, in particular, that the gift of speaking in tongues should be restrained in public worship where no interpreter is forthcoming. (4) Nowhere in the New Testament are these more sensational manifestations of the Spirit's presence regarded as harbingers of spiritual quickening, following upon spiritual decline, in either individuals or communities. (5) Nowhere does the New Testament suggest that all Christians, even in apostolic times, experienced one or another of the more specific charismatic gifts. All Christians have some gift, we are told, but not all have the gifts of healing, or of working miracles, or of speaking with tongues (compare I Cor. 12: 4–11 with verses 28–30). (6) Nowhere does the New Testament give us direct encouragement to seek the gift of speaking in tongues, or to regard ourselves as spiritually inferior and substandard if we lack it, or to imagine that enjoyment of it guarantees spiritual advance. The Corinthians, who apparently took an excessive interest in these particular manifestations, seem to have been the most disorderly, immoral, and immature church to which Paul ever wrote!

It is not for us to deny that in particular situations God may revive special manifestations of this kind. But we need to insist, first, that there is no biblical warrant for specially desiring such a revival; second, that there is no biblical warrant for thinking that, even if such a revival took place, it would be very important; third, that Scripture gives us no basis, in either precept or promise, for asking God to bestow such special abilities on all alike; fourth, that those who lay claim to their possession should not wonder if others find it necessary to submit their claim to fairly searching interrogation; fifth, that the distinctive new covenant ministries of the Spirit are neither furthered by the giving of such manifestations nor impeded by the withdrawing or withholding of them. Their purpose, according to the New Testament, was *dispensational* rather than personal; that is, they were given to authenticate the Gospel and its first messengers, and to mark publicly the transition from the era of the old covenant to that of the new. The need for them ended when the apostles' unique ministry was finished and the writing of the New Testament was completed. They provided special supernatural confirmation of the divine origin of 'the faith which was once for all delivered to the saints' (Jude 3). But such a period of God's special intervention in history can no more be reproduced now than the incarnation itself can happen a second time. We are of course not wishing to deny that this class of gifts, when given, may in certain cases have served under God to further believers' communion with the glorified Christ or to advance the work of grace in their hearts. But however true this may be, it does not alter the fact that this was not their main purpose, nor were they actually needed for this purpose. To suggest that any subjective spiritual enrichment is necessarily dependent now upon the fresh granting of such manifestations would be a serious mistake.

### BAPTISM WITH THE SPIRIT

What we are saying then comes to this. At Pentecost the Holy Spirit of Christ, 'the promise of the Father' (Acts 1: 4), the gift promised through the prophet Joel for the 'last days', was 'poured out' (Acts 2: 17), so that the disciples were 'filled' (Acts 2: 4). In this way Jesus 'baptized' them with the Holy Spirit and endued them with 'power from on high', just as He had said He would (Lk. 24: 49; Acts 1: 5). What this meant was that suddenly and powerfully, to the accompaniment of a sound like wind and a vision of tongues of fire, the Spirit began to overwhelm them with a clear and vivid realization of the glory of their glorified Saviour, to intoxicate them with a thrilling sense of His love and power towards them, and to make it impossible for them to keep quiet; they had to talk about Jesus, they could not stop themselves! Inhibitions were gone; spontaneously, that which filled their hearts with ecstasy and joy overflowed into speech. Thus the distinctive new covenant ministry of the Spirit began—and began, we may add, in the fullest strength! Though the disciples were regenerate, and their sins were forgiven, and they had already known something of the Spirit's ministry prior to Pentecost (see Jn. 14: 17), this was their first introduction to the full and characteristic experience of new covenant Christianity. As such, it was in truth their 'baptism' (the image is essentially initiatory) in the Holy Spirit. The water-baptism of John (the source of this image: see Mt. 3: 11, Mk. 1: 8, Lk. 3: 16, Jn. 1: 33, Acts 1: 5, 11: 16) initiated penitents into the expectant community, the company of those who, having turned from sin, were awaiting the coming Messiah; but the Spirit-baptism of Christ initiated believers into the life of glory, the experience of realized fellowship with the Messiah who had come, died, risen, and was now glorified at God's right hand.

On that day the disciples to whom the Spirit was first given spoke in tongues, but this was not, so far as one can judge, an integral element in the 'baptism'. The same 'baptism' was promised to, and seemingly received by, the three thousand converts (Acts 2: 38), but there is no hint that all these spoke with tongues. In I Corinthians 12 Paul shows that he, for one, did not expect that all those whom Christ had baptized with the one Spirit into the one body would speak in tongues (compare vv. 13 and 30).

Inevitably at that particular point of time at which the new covenant dispensation of grace replaced the old, some of those 'baptized' with the Holy Spirit were persons who had for some time been regenerate. Such, we saw, were Jesus' own disciples, and such too, no doubt, were some of the 'devout men' (Acts 2: 5) whom Peter's Pentecost sermon led to faith in the crucified Jesus as the risen and reigning Christ. The same should perhaps be said of Cornelius, another 'devout man' (cf. Acts 10: 2–4), and of the Ephesian 'disciples' who knew only John's message and baptism (19: 1–5). The special manifestations in both these latter instances showed that the post-pentecostal rule was in operation—the rule, namely, that the new covenant gift and ministry of the Spirit to believers, of which the special manifestations were an outward sign, dates from the moment when He leads them to faith in the glorified Jesus.

The case of the Samaritan converts spoken of in Acts 8 seems therefore not to be parallel to these, for here were persons whom Christ had undoubtedly baptized with the Spirit when they first believed and received water-baptism in His name. Their subsequent 'receiving' of the Holy Spirit (vv. 15, 17, 19) would appear to have had to do only with the special manifestations, attesting God's reception of them into the same new covenant community into which Jewish believers had come. Note that in Acts 8: 16 the record says that the Spirit 'had not yet *fallen on* any of them'. The point of this phraseology apparently is not that no one had received the promised gift of the indwelling Spirit, but that no one had experienced any accompanying special manifestations. (Cf. Acts 10: 44; 11: 15. For further comment on this incident see p. 42f. below.) However this may be, what is clear is that God has established by promise a direct connection, both theological and chronological, between repentance and faith in Christ on the one hand, and the new covenant gift and ministry of the Spirit on the other. Therefore all who have come to faith in Christ since the day of Pentecost, without a single exception, have been 'baptized' by Him in the Spirit into the one body and 'made to drink of one Spirit' (I Cor. 12: 13)—that is, the glorified Lord has sent His Spirit to indwell them, and to do within them His characteristic new covenant work. This means then that all who are 'born of the Spirit' (Jn. 3: 6) are also 'baptized in the Spirit'. The concepts of Spirit-birth and Spirit-baptism, though not identical, express two aspects of a single reality—new creation in Christ—and thus belong inseparably together. Some, no doubt, have failed to appreciate the gift that has been given them, as we suggested earlier, and have behaved in a way that has actually quenched the Spirit; but that is another issue, which for the moment we must leave aside.

## ASKING FOR THE SPIRIT

An objection might be raised at this point. We read that Jesus said: 'If you then, who are evil, know how to give good gifts to your children, how much more will the heavenly Father give the Holy Spirit to those who ask him' (Lk. 11: 13). Does this not envisage children of God in a state where they lack the gift of the Spirit, and need to ask specifically for it? Two points may be made in reply. The first is that these words must not be interpreted out of their historical context. They were spoken to the disciples before Pentecost, to encourage them to look forward to, and start praying for, the pentecostal 'good gift' which, as Jesus knew, their heavenly Father willed in due course to give them. But all who have become Christians since Pentecost have received this 'good gift' at the outset, and do not need therefore to ask for it. The second point is that it is not in any case warrantable to limit the phrase 'give the Holy Spirit' to the moment of initial donation. For God's giving is compared to earthly parents giving good gifts (plural) to their children. Just as those once 'filled' with the Spirit may be 'filled' again and again, to meet the demands of new situations (cf. Acts 2: 4; 4: 8, 31), so those, to whom the Spirit has once been given, may surely be 'given the Holy Spirit' again and again, in the sense of experiencing repeatedly the truth that 'he gives more grace' (Jas. 4: 6). The phrase 'give the Holy Spirit' denotes, not just a single momentary event, but the sustained experience of the Spirit's ministry. So Christians may pray repeatedly that God will 'give them the Holy Spirit' to make them equal to specific tests and tasks without thereby throwing doubt on the once-for-all bestowal of the indwelling Spirit at the time when they first came to faith.

CHAPTER FIVE

# RECEIVING THE SPIRIT

On the divine side the primary truth about receiving the Spirit is that Christ the Lord is Himself the sole giver, and that individuals who would receive this gift must have direct dealings with Him. On the human side, the primary truth is that the one indispensable condition for the reception of the Spirit is personal faith in Christ.

### RECEPTION IS BY FAITH

So when Jesus proclaimed, 'If any one thirst, let him come to me and drink. He who believes in me, as the scripture has said, "Out of his heart shall flow rivers of living water",' the evangelist's comment was, 'Now this he said about the Spirit, *which those who believed in him were to receive*' (Jn. 7: 37f.).

Commenting to the Jerusalem church on his experience in the house of Cornelius, when the Spirit was given to those who had simply heard the word preached, Peter said, 'God gave the same gift to them as he gave to us when we believed in the Lord Jesus Christ' (Acts 11: 17). He repeated this testimony at the council of Jerusalem. 'God made choice among you', he said, 'that by my mouth the Gentiles should hear the word of the gospel and believe. And God who knows the heart bore witness to them, giving them the Holy Spirit just as he did to us; and he made no distinction between us and them, but cleansed their hearts by faith' (Acts 15: 7-9).

Nor is Paul's teaching any different. When the Galatian Christians were disturbed by false teaching, he wrote, 'Let me ask you only this: Did you receive the Spirit by works of the law, or by hearing with faith?' (Gal. 3: 2). Here Paul treats reception of the Spirit as one aspect of the decisive initiating event by which they became Christians, and implies by the form of his question that it took place when they heard the Word and believed. In the same chapter we actually find him saying: 'Christ redeemed us ... that we might *receive the promise of the Spirit through faith*' (Gal. 3: 13f.).

Similarly, Paul reminds the Ephesians that they received the Spirit when they heard the Gospel and believed in the Saviour. To quote: 'In him [that is, in Christ] you also, who have heard the word of truth, the gospel of your salvation, and have believed in him, were sealed with the promised Holy Spirit' (Eph. 1: 13). 'Sealing' is a sign by which ownership is attested and assured. This 'sealing' has sometimes been understood as an inward act of the Spirit assuring us of salvation, which may not occur till a long time after conversion. Grammatically, however, the Spirit is not here the sealer, but the seal; it is the gift of the indwelling Spirit, as such, that is God's assurance to us that we are His; and there are no grounds for separating this assuring gift from the moment of faith. Indeed, it is impossible to do so; for 'any one who does not have the Spirit of Christ does not belong to him' (Rom. 8: 9).

## THE WAY TO FAITH

But what is the faith, the 'believing', of which we have been speaking so freely? Not just cosmic optimism, nor simply intellectual assent to the doctrine of the Creed, but rather personal confidence in, and committal of oneself to, the risen Lord. It is equated in John 1: 12 with *receiving* Him: that is, acknowledging Him as all that He claims to be, and on that basis welcoming Him as one's divine Saviour and Master. Such faith is said to issue in being born of God; which is another way of indicating that such faith leads to reception of the life-giving Spirit.

If therefore we are to help those who know nothing of the indwelling of the Spirit to receive this gift from God, what is needed in the first place is not that we should offer them the sacraments of the Church, but that we should preach to them the Gospel of Christ, so that we may lead them to face their sin and need, to renounce all self-help and self-confidence, and to put their whole and sole trust in the Saviour. The highest prominence needs to be given, more so than is always done in Anglicanism, to what St. Paul calls 'the word of faith which we preach' (Rom. 10: 8).

We may learn what such ministry meant and led to in Paul's work for God from his description of the way in which the Christians at Thessalonica entered into the experience of salvation in Christ. To them he wrote, 'But we are bound to give thanks to God always for you, brethren beloved by the Lord, because God chose you from the beginning to be saved, through sanctification by the Spirit and *belief in the truth*. To this *he called you through our gospel*' (II Thess. 2: 13f.). Salvation became theirs in personal experience through the work of the Spirit on God's side, and the response of faith on man's side; and this response was prompted when they heard God calling them to faith in Christ through Paul's preaching of the Gospel.

In the light of this it is worth asking whether in these days we achieve the right emphasis in our confirmation services. Our desire is that candidates should through confirmation receive an increase of the sanctifying Spirit. But if this is to be, then it is surely plain that what we need is a greater place for the faithful preaching of the word of salvation, and less prominence for the bishop and his laying on of hands. The bishop is not the object of faith, nor his hand the channel of grace, and it is the spiritually present Christ, not the physically present bishop, on whom attention should be focused. In confirmation and elsewhere it is high time that Christ and the Gospel should increase and the bishop and episcopal ceremonial decrease; at least, it is high time that they should if we wish to see new life from God appear in our churches.

### THE PLACE OF BAPTISM

In saying this, however, we anticipate the answer to our next question, which many by now will be wanting to raise. How do baptism and confirmation fit into the scheme? What is their positive relation to God's gift of the Spirit?

The first thing to say is that reception of the Spirit is rightly associated with baptism, because baptism with water is the divinely-appointed sign and seal of the baptism of the Spirit. Just as Christian baptism is an acted symbol which speaks of cleansing from sin, of justification before God in Christ crucified and risen, and of incorporation into Christ's body, the Church, so, in its richness of significance, it speaks also of the baptism of the Spirit. But it only symbolizes and pledges these benefits as a sign, seal, and token of them. It does not of itself bestow them. Only Christ does that, and He does it in response to the faith of the candidate. In order therefore to enjoy the divine gifts which, as his baptism solemnly and personally assures him, are meant for him, the person baptized must confess faith in Christ, and call upon His name as Saviour and Lord.

A direct parallel is provided by the Jewish rite of circumcision, and by Paul's explanation of its place and significance. It was, he says, a sign and seal of God's gift of righteousness. As such it was given to Abraham after he believed, and to his descendants in infancy before they believed. But in each case the gift signified was received immediately, and only, when the individual concerned believed. Abraham therefore received the gift of righteousness before he was circumcised, when he believed; and his descendants received it not when they were circumcised but when they followed Abraham's example and personally believed in God and in His word of promise. (See Rom. 4: 9-12.)

Would that the corresponding significance of baptism and the decisive necessity of faith were similarly explained and understood in more of our churches! Then many, who now do not see, might come to see that it is not participating in the ceremony of baptism, as such, that makes salvation and the gift of the Spirit ours. Nor does it matter, from this standpoint, whether an individual is baptized in infancy before believing, or in adult life after believing. What matters supremely, and what determines whether the promised benefits become his or not, is his personal faith in the risen Lord. In New Testament times it was taken for granted that baptism and faith would always go together, so that where you found the former you would find the latter too. The apostles constantly exhort their readers on this basis. If only the same could be taken for granted today!

### THE SIGNIFICANCE OF CONFIRMATION

It is as a means of maintaining this connection between baptism and faith that the Prayer Book use of confirmation should be seen. It is this purpose, rather than any recorded precedent, that constitutes its biblical basis and warrant. Since personal repentance and faith are indispensable for all who would enjoy the benefits which baptism pledges, our Reformers were concerned to ensure that all who were baptized in infancy should be brought to appreciate the necessity of this personal response, and helped, when they become old enough to make a responsible choice, both to decide and publicly to confess their determination to turn from sin, and to trust in and follow the Saviour. Hence the Catechism and the confirmation service.

This personal confession of faith on the part of the candidate is in fact the most important part of the confirmation ceremony. It is the direct basis on which his admission to holy communion rests. If we wish to see an increase of genuine Christian experience and consecration in our churches, then this part of every person's confirmation must be given its proper prominence and importance. More could be done to this end than we do at the moment. It would be good for every candidate to be called on by name, and to have to answer as an individual, in the presence of the congregation, the same detailed questions that his godparents or sureties answered for him at his baptism.

The prayer then offered for him by the bishop and congregation needs careful appreciation also. Our Prayer Book does not direct the bishop to ask for the Spirit to be given for the first time, as if the candidate had not previously received Him. Indeed, when he lays his hands on the candidate's head he does not ask for any gift of the Spirit from above at all. Rather, having heard the candidate's personal confession of faith, the bishop treats him as a child of God already, and therefore as one who has already received the Spirit, because he has himself believed in Christ; and so he prays that the candidate may daily increase in the Holy Spirit more and more—that is, that the fruit of the indwelling Spirit, who is already his, may be increasingly manifested in his life.[1]

It is noticeable that a Prayer Book rubric allows that a person prevented from sharing in a confirmation service may none the less come to the holy communion, provided he 'be ready and desirous to be confirmed'. This is a further indication that the decisive factor which qualifies a man for communicant status is not the episcopal laying on of hands, as such, but his personal repentance, faith, and obedience.

### THE USE OF THE LAYING ON OF HANDS

To lay hands on an individual while prayer is offered for him is simply a visible indication to all concerned that this is the person for whom the blessing specified is desired. This was what the laying on of hands by Peter and John meant at Samaria, when they prayed that those who had already believed and been baptized in the name of the Lord Jesus might 'receive the Holy Spirit'. They did this only because there was as yet no visible sign, such as the special manifestations had been among the Jewish Christians, that the Spirit had been given to them. 'For it had not yet fallen on any of them' (see Acts 8: 14–17). Also, in those particular circumstances, in which some doubtless questioned whether God meant Samaritans to share in the blessings of Christ, it was desirable that decisive and immediately recognizable evidence should be given, if God were

---

[1] For an impressive refutation of modern attempts to represent confirmation as the decisive means whereby the Spirit is given, see G. W. H. Lampe: *The Seal of the Spirit* (London, 1951).

pleased to grant it. This may therefore be what the apostles prayed for—some outward sign showing that the Spirit had been given, such as would be afforded by them prophesying or speaking with tongues (cf. Acts 19: 5f.).

The circumstances on this occasion may indicate why, in this special case, the bestowal of these special manifestations was delayed—namely, in order that Peter and John might be present as witnesses to see the incontrovertible evidence that God intended Samaritans equally to share in the gift of the Spirit. It is at least noteworthy in this connection that on their return journey to Jerusalem Peter and John preached the Gospel to many villages of the Samaritans (Acts 8: 25). In any case, since this was clearly by any standards an abnormal occasion, it would be unjustifiable to argue from it that the special laying on of hands by bishops, or anyone else, subsequent to baptism is normally necessary for the reception of the Spirit, in any sense of that phrase, by those who have believed in Christ. When the 1928 Confirmation Service declares that 'in ministering Confirmation the Church doth follow the example of the Apostles', and goes on, after quoting this narrative, to say, 'The Scripture here teacheth us that a special gift of the Holy Spirit is bestowed through laying on of hands with prayer', it makes a profound blunder.

It is recorded that Paul laid hands on the twelve 'disciples' at Ephesus immediately following their baptism. Presumably he prayed for them also, in terms similar to those in which Peter and John prayed at Samaria. But there is no evidence that Paul did this regularly to all whom he baptized. There is, for instance, no suggestion that in Philippi Paul laid his hands on Lydia or on the jailer at the time of their baptism; and it would be absurd to suggest that because of such an omission they, or others like them, never received the Spirit! Similarly there is no indication that the three thousand converts on the day of Pentecost, or the Ethiopian eunuch, had hands laid on them after their baptism.

In this connection we must weigh the significance of the question which Paul put to the Ephesian 'disciples' when first he met them. What he asked them was, 'Did you receive the Holy Spirit when you believed?' (Acts 19: 1f.). Such a question both indicates that it is through personal faith that the Spirit is received, and also, by consequence, implies that, if a person has not received the Spirit, his faith cannot be full Christian faith. This is exactly what Paul found to be the case here. These men had shared only in John's baptism, not in baptism into Christ. Evidently they only knew John's message. They were strictly in a pre-Christian situation. So Paul preached to them Christ crucified and glorified. They believed, and 'were baptized in the name of the Lord Jesus'. Then the special manifestations were given, so making it plain that these men, too, had received the gift of the indwelling Spirit, and had been accepted by Christ into the new covenant fellowship.

THE PRACTICAL ISSUE

Imagine a house in which a main water supply is laid on, but strangely never used; and whose occupants continue to wait —and sometimes to send a flurry of urgent requests to the Water Board!—for supplies of water to be provided for them. Such is the state of many Christians regarding the Holy Spirit. They are seeking, often with desperate seriousness, a gift which they already have. Nor is it only unenlightened individuals who do this. The Church at large has inherited from the past, and frequently and solemnly uses in the present, hymns like, 'Come Holy Ghost, our souls inspire'. The late Professor J. E. L. Oulton of Dublin rightly says in his book *Holy Communion and Holy Spirit* that Christians of the early centuries would never have thought of praying such a prayer, for the knowledge that God had already given them His Holy Spirit was clear in their minds. The most they ever prayed was 'Take not Thy Holy Spirit from us'[2]—a rather different emphasis!

In this connection we may quote the apt words of H. B.

---

[2] See J. E. L. Oulton: *Holy Communion and Holy Spirit* (London, 1951), pp. 130–135.

Swete, 'Moreover the attitude of the primitive Church towards the Spirit was rather one of joyful welcome than of invocation; the cry *Veni, Creator Spiritus* belongs to a later age, when the Spirit was sought and perhaps expected, but not regarded as a guest who had already come, and come to abide'.[3] So if by accustomed use we continue to sing such words as 'Come, Holy Ghost' they must be understood not as a prayer for the fresh arrival of One who is absent, but as a request for the present activity towards us and within us of One who is already present and dwelling within our hearts.

The truth to which many true Christians urgently need to be awakened is that God has already given His Spirit to them. Paul would wish to say to us all, as he said to the Christians in Corinth, 'Do you not know that your body is a temple of the Holy Spirit within you, which you have from God?' (I Cor. 6: 19).

If we are Christ's, we need not seek for the baptism of the Spirit as an experience yet to become ours. Rather we must face the demand that we act in the light of what we have already, and set ourselves to work out our own salvation with fear and trembling, remembering that God by His Spirit is already at work in us both to will and to work for His good pleasure. (See Phil. 2: 12f.)

---

[3] H. B. Swete: *The Holy Spirit in the New Testament* (London, 1909), p. 96.

CHAPTER SIX

# WALKING BY THE SPIRIT

If we are Christ's, we have already been given the indwelling Spirit with all the rich possibilities of new life and fruitfulness that this gift promises. What then must we do to enjoy a full outworking of the new life in experience? In the present chapter we shall review some of the main points that arise when one attempts to answer this question.

## LIBERTY

The most convenient starting-point is the New Testament insistence that the Gospel brings *freedom*. 'Where the Spirit of the Lord is, there is liberty' (II Cor. 3: 17, A.V.). When God's Son sets men free, they become free indeed (Jn. 8: 36). Paul writes to the Galatian Christians, 'You were called to freedom' (Gal. 5: 13); 'For freedom Christ has set us free' (Gal. 5: 1). Christ has liberated us from sin (Rom. 6: 17f.), the law (Gal. 4: 21ff.), Satan (Mk. 3: 27; Jn. 12: 31f.), and the fear of death (Heb. 2: 15)—so, instead of a life of legalistic religion, moral failure, and inward disquiet and unease, those to whom Christ gives His Spirit are introduced into the freedom of God's family—the 'liberty of the children of God' (Rom. 8: 21). 'The Spirit you have received is not a spirit of slavery leading you back into a life of fear, but a Spirit that makes us sons, enabling us to cry "Abba! Father!"' (8: 15, N.E.B.). As children of God, says Paul, we are brothers of Christ and heirs of His glory—and this is freedom indeed.

Our liberty is both *external* and *internal*. *Externally*, our relation to God's law, and to the God whose law it is, is changed. No longer do we have to live as those who, for want of any better alternative, must seek righteousness and acceptance with God as a reward for work done, and must fear divine rejection every moment for our moral shortcomings. Instead, we live in the liberating knowledge that Christ has settled all the law's claims against us, and that we are now fully accepted for His sake. *Internally* our nature and heart's attitude to God are changed; for sin—the anti-God impulse which was previously our ruling 'drive'—is dethroned, and our deepest urge henceforth is to seek, and love, and know, and serve, and praise, and please, God. This is the first and decisive step in God's work of ironing out the moral distortions and twists that have marred His image in us hitherto. It is the deepest element in that inward work of grace which makes Christians so radically different from the rest of men—the work which Christ called new birth of the Spirit (Jn. 3: 3ff.), and which Paul described as co-resurrection with Christ (Rom. 6: 5–14; Col. 2: 12f.; 3: 1), new creation in Christ (II Cor. 5: 17), and regeneration and renewing in the Holy Spirit (Tit. 3: 5).

What then is the nature of the Christian's relation to God, and to His law, henceforth? Paradoxically—yet none the less naturally and inevitably for that—it is a relation of *free bond-service*. Freely—that is, voluntarily, deliberately, and wholeheartedly—those whom Christ has freed enslave themselves afresh to God (Rom. 6: 17–22), to Christ (I Cor. 7: 22), to righteousness (Rom. 6: 18), and to all their fellow-men for Christ's sake and the Gospel's sake (II Cor. 4: 5; I Cor. 9: 19–23). Christian liberty, it appears, is neither an invitation to irresponsibility nor a sanctioning of licence. The fact that Christians are no longer 'under law' (Rom. 6: 14) for salvation does not mean that they are therefore 'without law toward God' (I Cor. 9: 21). Rather, as Paul goes straight on to say, they are 'under the law of Christ'—that is, out of love to their Saviour, whose cross is the measure of His love to them, they henceforth live 'no longer for themselves but for him who for their sake died and was raised' (II Cor. 5: 15). They show their love to Christ by seeking to fulfill 'the law of Christ' (Gal. 6: 2). And this is something which they not merely ought to do, but want to do; for those who have had the laws of God written on their hearts in regeneration (see Heb. 8: 10) find that they love, not merely Christ Himself, but His commands too. In the regenerate life, Christ's will and our heart's desire come increasingly to coincide. So His service remains 'perfect freedom'—for in serving Him we are doing the thing which, in our heart of hearts, we most want to do, and which yields us a joy and satisfaction and contentment more profound than any the unregenerate can ever know. What truer or more perfect freedom can there be than that?

The position, then, is that, just as Christ's service is perfect freedom, so the maintained experience of perfect freedom depends upon diligence in serving Christ.

### LEGALISM AND LICENCE

Not all Christians, however, realize the truth and significance of these facts, and the danger of slipping back through inadvertence or negligence into bondage of one sort or another is constantly present. Paul finds it necessary to give warning that the true enjoyment of Christian freedom requires continual vigilance against perils on both sides. On the one hand, he writes, 'Stand fast therefore, and do not submit again to a yoke of slavery' (Gal. 5: 1): and on the other hand, 'Do not use your freedom as an opportunity for the flesh', or 'Do not turn your freedom into licence for your lower nature' (Gal. 5: 13, R.S.V. and N.E.B.). The first warning is against relapsing into a legalistic form of religion, in which one's acceptance with God is thought to depend directly upon law-keeping. To relapse in this way (as the Galatians were in effect being tempted to do by the circumcision party) is to forfeit one's Spirit-given liberty in its external aspect. The second warning is against self-indulgent licence, which is both an abuse of Christian liberty in its external aspect and a real renouncing of it in its internal aspect; for it is a surrendering of oneself to be mastered by sin once more.

These warnings are still needed, for these perils still beset us. On the one hand many are prevented, by forms of legalism or traditionalism which hold them in unhealthy bondage, from enjoying true liberty in the Spirit. Having lapsed into the superstitious notion that certain religious routines are, not merely a beneficial means of further grace, but actually an essential condition of their continued standing in God's favour, their life comes to be overshadowed by fear of the consequences of omitting them, and the joy of the knowledge of full acceptance and adoption for Christ's sake alone does not come their way. This is an evil.

On the other hand there are those who have felt the force of the truth that we are accepted, not because of what we are or have done, but because Christ in mercy died for our sins. These are constantly tempted to take advantage of their freedom from 'the terrors of law' to engage in activities which are more of the flesh than of the Spirit, and which satisfy self rather than promote God's glory or edify men. This also is an evil.

True liberty is not easily enjoyed and preserved. We need to learn how to possess it properly, and to resist the inclination to treat it as sanctioning licence. Jude's warning against those who 'pervert the grace of our God into licentiousness' (Jude 4) is a word always in season. For we still have within us all the tendencies to sinful self-indulgence which we had before we were Christians. Sin, though dethroned in us, is not eradicated from us, and the 'lusts of the flesh', though quiescent perhaps for a time, are still very much present with us. What God said to Cain when he began to hate Abel may be applied directly to all of us all the time: 'Sin is couching at the door; its desire is for you, but *you must master it*' (Gen. 4: 7).

A car facing up a slope is bound to run backwards downhill, once the brakes are taken off, unless its engine drives it the other way. The thrust of the engine causes the vehicle to move in an opposite direction to that in which the downward pull of its own weight would otherwise have taken it—assuming, of course, that the driver keeps its nose pointing uphill, and does not let it veer out of course. So the Christian who sets himself, as it were, to move uphill, finds that by the power of the indwelling Spirit he can actually do so.

Freedom from the indwelling sin-principle which otherwise

takes me captive (see Rom. 7: 23) will be enjoyed, and the righteous standards of God's law will increasingly be fulfilled, by those who 'walk'—that is, move forward—'not according to the flesh but according to the Spirit' (see Rom. 8: 4). 'Walk by the Spirit, and ye shall not fulfil the lust of the flesh' (Gal. 5: 16, R.V.).

### CO-OPERATING ACTIVITY

So the enjoyment of true liberty in the Spirit, the enjoyment, that is, of practical victory over the flesh and of genuine progress in holy living, is impossible without our co-operating activity. It is our privilege and responsibility, so to speak, to drive the car, and by our own deliberate and sustained choice to direct it uphill and not down. For God's gift to us of new life in Christ makes this activity possible on our part, as it never was before. Objectively, by regeneration, Christians, 'having been set free from sin, *have become* slaves of righteousness' (Rom. 6: 18). The practical application, stated in the next verse, is: '*now yield* your members to righteousness for sanctification'. In other words, act according to what is now your real nature; *be* what you *are*; be *yourself!* The epistles of the New Testament are full of urgent exhortations to Christians to begin to move in this new direction, living out what God has wrought in them, by the power of the indwelling Spirit.

Just here, as we observed earlier, many true Christians who are eager to enjoy victory over sin and to progress in holiness make a grievous mistake. They become passive. Knowing their own natural inability and their proneness to fail and to fall, they are afraid to venture forward. Fearing that any initiative on their part, even in obeying the direct injunctions of God, would be the energy of the flesh, they wait for God to move them by a direct inner impulse before they will do anything. What they ought to do is to show, by a disciplined boldness in acting on God's commands, their confidence in the presence and power of the indwelling Spirit, who is given to support and enable them once they begin to move forward in the right way.

So Paul challenges and exhorts Christians: 'If we live by the Spirit, let us also walk by the Spirit' (Gal. 5: 25). 'Walk by the Spirit, and ye shall not fulfil the lust of the flesh' (Gal. 5: 16, R.V.). He demands that we co-operate with God, and thus make it possible for His inward work to find expression in our outward lives, so that we move forward constantly under the Spirit's constraint in the pathway of faith and obedience. 'Work out your own salvation', Paul writes: 'for God is at work in you, both to will and to work for his good pleasure' (Phil. 2: 12f.).

### OBEDIENCE

It is only in the pathway of obedience that the active co-operation of the Spirit is experienced. Think of an electrically driven trolley-bus. It is not on rails like a train. The driver has all the time to follow the appointed route by his own active observation and deliberate choice. He could, if he chose, at a crossroads, take a wrong turning. But if he did he would immediately lose the supply of electricity from the overhead wires; for they are laid on only along the appointed route, and not along every road. So many who are God's children do not enjoy the full benefit of His Spirit's presence and power simply because they have not kept to His way. Their immediate need is not fresh enduement from above but a radical re-ordering of their personal lives, so that they begin to co-operate with the Spirit instead of—to use the New Testament terms—'resisting', 'grieving', and 'quenching' Him (Acts 7: 51; Eph. 4: 30; I Thess. 5: 19).

### RIGHT USE OF THE MIND

This re-ordering must begin, St. Paul teaches, in the realm of the mind. 'Do not be conformed', he writes, 'to this world but be transformed *by the renewal of your mind*, that you may prove what is the will of God, what is good and acceptable and perfect' (Rom. 12: 2). The Gospel, as he reminds us elsewhere, summoned us 'to be renewed in the spirit of your mind', as part of the wider requirement 'that ye put on the new man, which after God is created in righteousness and true holiness' (Eph. 4: 23f., A.V.).

We ourselves decisively determine the course which we follow and the character which we develop by the kind of interests and occupations to which we choose to give our minds. For, as Paul says, 'those who live according to the flesh set their minds on the things of the flesh, but those who live according to the Spirit set their minds on the things of the Spirit' (Rom. 8: 5). The determining choice is ours. God has given us His Spirit, and now waits for us to 'be what we are' by properly giving our minds to spiritual things.

### SCRIPTURES WRITTEN FOR OUR INSTRUCTION

Clearly, if we are to do this we need a text-book for study, and a guide-book for directions. And God has provided one. This is exactly why the Scriptures were written—namely, to provide our minds with the knowledge and guidance, both positive and negative, that we need, if we are to steer our course rightly. 'All scripture is inspired by God and profitable for teaching, for reproof, for correction, and for training in righteousness, that the man of God may be complete, equipped for every good work' (II Tim. 3: 16f.; see also Rom. 15: 4).

So regular, diligent study of God's written Word, both personal and corporate, is indispensable for all who would walk in God's way, and thus experience more of the Spirit's power. Nor will the kind of academic literary and historical study of the Bible which is detached from life, and in which the students themselves act simply as interested observers, fill the bill. Bible study must be applicatory in spirit and intention. In an age in which applicatory exposition of Scripture from our pulpits scarcely exists, and 'scientific' Bible study normally limits its aim to the securing of historical and theological correctness, the need for Bible study to be *practical* cannot be too strongly stated. Bible study must be undertaken with a positive readiness to receive through it direct guidance from God concerning our own personal faith and conduct. Only so shall we come to 'understand what the will of the Lord is', and to be preserved from the folly of expecting God to prosper our mistaken choices and unwise courses (see Eph. 5: 15-17).

As we give ourselves to the study of God's Word, we shall begin at once to experience the benefit of the indwelling Spirit's co-operating action. For if as we study we are willing to learn and to be led, the Spirit will become our teacher and enlighten and increase our understanding, so that more and more we shall discern what we should believe, and how we should act to please God. As Jesus Himself said, 'If any man's will is to do his will, he shall *know* whether the teaching is from God' (Jn. 7: 17).

No one can grow up to become a mature man of God unless he is willing to be taught and disciplined in the school of the Spirit. Bible students must be ready for the Spirit to confront them with personal reproof and the need for correction. We have many shortcomings and positive faults. Nor can we be made completely holy and perfect overnight. Whatever crises it may involve for particular persons in particular circumstances, sanctification—the changing of us into the likeness of Christ—is fundamentally a process, lasting the whole of life, and no single 'experience', or 'blessing', second, third, fourth, or fourteenth —number it how you will—can cancel the need for God's daily discipline of corrective training. If we are to make progress in holy living, it is essential that we constantly expose ourselves to what II Tim. 3: 16 (quoted above) called 'training in righteousness', and to those dealings whereby God 'disciplines us for our good, that we may share his holiness' (see Heb. 12: 5-11).

### DISCRIMINATION

Equally necessary, if we are to grow up to full spiritual manhood, and increase in practical holiness, are 'faculties trained by practice to distinguish good from evil'—the distinguishing mark of the truly mature (see Heb. 5: 14).

In making us by grace sons in His family, God means us to

acquire the capacity for Christian moral decision, as individuals who are fully and personally responsible and able to choose for ourselves. The extent to which a man's capacity for responsible, discriminating personal choice has developed is one measure of his growth in grace. Prudence, and wise discernment, are among the gifts of the Spirit. Consequently one of Paul's prayers for his converts was that their love might 'abound more and more, with knowledge and all discernment', so that they might be able to distinguish things that differ and to prefer the best, or 'approve what is excellent' (see Phil. 1: 9-11).

Christian living in this world is both dangerous and demanding. For it cannot be strictly governed by a fixed list of 'dos' and 'don'ts'—rules which decide beforehand how to act in every situation. The ideal of having rules for literally everything was part of the pharisaic vision of the good life, which our Lord rejected. The suggestion of the 'new moralists', that Jesus prescribed nothing at all save the motive of love, is certainly an incorrect report of His teaching; yet it is evident that Jesus understood the keeping of God's law in terms not of a mechanical observance of rules but of a discriminating application of principles and ideals, whereby one seeks constantly to 'make something' of situations for the good of men and the glory of God. From this point of view Christian living is not at all like driving a car through a big and busy town where hosts of traffic lights, road signs, lane markings and policemen crowd upon you to tell you at each point just what you must and must not do. Rather, Christian living is like steering a ship across a wide ocean where there are no highways or landmarks or traffic lights, and where the right course can be found and followed only by constant watchfulness and by acquired skill in navigation. The indwelling Spirit and the divinely inspired 'chart' of God's written Word are given to us to enable us to acquire and exercise this skill.

Some imagine that if the Spirit were fully ours, sensational guidance (by dreams, visions, voices, abnormal inward impressions, and such like) would be regularly experienced. But Scripture and Christian experience show that sensational guidance is not a normal or a frequent thing. Even for extraordinary men, chosen for extraordinary vocations, like Abraham, Elijah, or Paul, such experiences were the reverse of ordinary, or common. Such exceptional disclosures may be given at the beginning to establish someone in the faith, as in the case of Christ's initial appearances to Paul (see Acts 22: 6ff.); or they may be given at some decisive crisis to ensure that the right way is chosen and the wrong avoided, as when Peter saw the great sheet (Acts 10: 9-29), or Paul the man of Macedonia (Acts 16: 9ff.). For some Christians, as for some (one cannot say, all) of the biblical prophets, momentous questions of vocation have from time to time been resolved by extraordinary modes of guidance. But the Bible does not encourage us ever to expect experiences of this kind. Its stress is rather on the fact that we are meant by the help of the Spirit, and by the use of our renewed and dedicated mind, increasingly informed by the Scriptures, to 'prove'—that is, to find out from experience, and by testing and reflection—'what is the will of God' (Rom. 12: 2) for us to follow in each particular situation. It was to help us do this that Jesus' sermons on the mount and on the plain, and many of His parables, were given us along with the ethical portions of the epistles; and we should recognize that a statement like 'do not be foolish, but understand what the will of the Lord is' (Eph. 5: 17) urgently summons us to their study. We shall have more to say of this in chapter eight, where we discuss guidance in detail.

### CONFLICT

Walking by the Spirit means—if we may mix metaphors—swimming against the stream. With the world, the flesh, and the devil against us we may not expect an easy or painless passage. Our bird's-eye view of the Christian way must therefore close on a note of warning. We must not under-estimate the forces against us. The devil is cunning: the world is insidious; the flesh (not just our grosser and more vicious passions, but pride and selfishness too) is so much part of us that to 'mortify' and 'crucify' it—which, according to Paul, Christians do, and must do (Rom. 8: 13; Gal. 5: 24)—is, as our Lord taught, like plucking out one's eye, or cutting off one's hand or foot. Self-denial can hurt, and the temptation to draw back from the ultimate in discipleship is strong. Moreover, the temptation recurs; we never say goodbye to it till we leave this world. If it ceases in one form it starts up in another. Thus the Christian constantly finds himself opposed, distracted, enervated, assaulted as he seeks to go forward with God. The Christian life has its low moments as well as its high spots. It is conventional in many quarters today to play down this grimmer side of Christian living, but such a policy is the reverse of wise. The man who gets into the way of assuming, or pretending, that his foes are not there is asking to be ambushed; sooner or later he will find that his spiritual life has become a second Glencoe. The only man who is safe is he who knows his enemy, and is able to detect his approach and to counter-attack.

But it is precisely this that the man who walks by the Spirit can do. Because he is sensitive to God and His will, he is sensitive to the approach of Satan, for whom, being a realist, he is constantly on the watch. (See Mt. 26: 41.) But just as he does not under-estimate his enemies, so he does not over-estimate them either. For he knows that sin's dominion over him has been broken, so that he need never fall victim to it when direct conflict comes; and therefore he goes out to battle with a high heart, expecting not defeat but victory. His confidence rests in the power of the indwelling Spirit, and of the Saviour with whom he maintains contact, and to whom he constantly looks, by prayer, as the assault begins. Nor is his hope vain. He proves in experience the truth of God's promises: 'Resist the devil *and he will flee from you*' (Jas. 4: 7); 'walk by the Spirit, *and ye shall not fulfil the lust of the flesh*' (Gal. 5: 16, R.V.).

### FUNCTIONING IN FELLOWSHIP

The one Spirit, who indwells every believer in Christ, gives them fellowship with the Father and Son. He also unites them in one body. Therefore, all who are fellow-sharers in the one Spirit are thereby related to one another in fellowship: we partake of a common life. This means that we can only fully enjoy our Christian heritage if we realize that we are meant to live and function in active fellowship not only with God, but also with one another. Life in the Spirit is not an experience to be enjoyed independently and privately by us each as separate individuals. God's best of benefit and blessing is something that Christians can only possess *together*.

This is illustrated by the Israelites' entrance into the promised land. Single individuals could not go in by themselves. Though Joshua and Caleb had the faith in God to enter from the first, they had to wait through the forty years spent in the wilderness till all Israel was ready to enter in together.

We shall have more to say regarding this principle of mutual dependence at a later stage. For the moment, we simply make the point that the extent of our success in walking by the Spirit will depend very largely on the use we make of the fellowship of the saints.

CHAPTER SEVEN

# THE FULNESS OF THE SPIRIT

In the New Testament various people are described as being full of the Spirit; and in Paul's letter to the Ephesians all alike are exhorted to 'be filled with the Spirit' (Eph. 5: 18). What does this phraseology mean? How does one come to be 'filled with the Spirit'? How may this condition be maintained? If we want, on the one hand, to enjoy God's best for our lives, and, on the other hand, to avoid being bewildered and, perhaps, misled by conflicting opinions, we must seek scriptural answers to these questions.

## WHAT 'TO BE FULL OF' MEANS

The description 'to be full of' means to be possessed and dominated by. This can be either a temporary or a permanent condition. The phrase is, for instance, used of disease; Luke describes a man as 'full of leprosy' (Lk. 5: 12). It can also be used of attitudes of spirit: a man may be 'full' of anger, hatred or envy. (See, e.g. Esth. 3: 5; Dan. 3: 19; Acts 19: 28.) These may well be merely temporary conditions. But if a person is described, say after his death, as having been 'full' of kindness or goodwill, the reference is clearly then to a more permanent and habitual characteristic.

As we have already observed, a wide variety of characters are spoken of as having been 'full of the Spirit'. In some cases, the phrase refers only to a temporary condition, which explains why they acted as they did on that particular occasion. So Elizabeth and Zacharias, the parents of John the Baptist, were 'filled with the Spirit' when they prophesied and voiced their feelings in words of spiritual joy and worship (see Lk. 1: 41ff. and 67ff.). On the day of Pentecost, the disciples in Jerusalem were 'all filled with the Holy Spirit', with the consequence that they 'began to speak in other tongues, as the Spirit gave them utterance' (Acts 2: 4). On a later occasion the same company of disciples, having prayed, 'were all filled with the Holy Spirit and spoke the word of God with boldness' (Acts 4: 29-31). What is meant in each of these passages is that on one particular occasion the individuals concerned came to be possessed and dominated by the Spirit in an extraordinary manner so that they acted in a way that was not merely beyond their natural powers, but beyond what God Himself enabled them to do for most of the time.

## MEN FULL OF THE SPIRIT

Other individuals, however, were 'full of the Spirit' in a different sense. In their case the phrase clearly describes a permanent characteristic. The God-given promise concerning John the Baptist was that 'he will be filled with the Holy Spirit, even from his mother's womb' (Lk. 1: 15). Also, when the Jerusalem church saw need to appoint men 'to serve tables', the apostles exhorted the rest to 'pick out ... seven men of good repute, full of the Spirit and of wisdom'; and Stephen, the first to be chosen, is personally described as 'a man full of faith and of the Holy Spirit' (see Acts 6: 1-6). Later, Barnabas is described as 'a good man, full of the Holy Spirit and of faith' (Acts 11: 24).

In these cases the phrase identifies an abiding characteristic. These individuals' lives were permanently possessed and dominated by the Spirit. His presence and influence were recognizable in everything they did; not only when they preached the word, but also when they served tables or gave friendly encouragement to fellow-Christians.

## 'LET THE HOLY SPIRIT FILL YOU'

To this abiding state of full possession and domination in every part of life by the indwelling Spirit Paul exhorts Christians when he writes, 'Be filled with the Spirit', or, 'Let the Holy

Spirit fill you' (Eph. 5: 18, R.S.V. and N.E.B.). The imperative 'Be filled' is in the present tense, implying continuous action. This is something we are told to be doing all the time—namely, to keep ourselves full. We keep our lungs full of fresh air by constantly breathing; we are to keep ourselves filled with the Spirit by constantly exposing ourselves to His active ministry towards us.

We should note that, in the nature of the case, 'fulness' is a relative term. Its measure and extent are determined at each moment by the existing area of emptiness, or capacity for intake; and this may vary. Thus, the patch used to cover a hole in a garment is described as 'its fulness', i.e. 'that which fills it up' (Mt. 9: 16, A.V.). Its actual size will depend upon the extent of the hole to be filled. A bigger 'fulness' may be needed next time! Now, imagine a doctor telling a patient that he is not using his lungs properly, and that he needs to learn to breathe more deeply. If the patient were like some seekers after the fulness of the Spirit, his immediate reaction would be to ask the doctor to produce his lung pump, and properly fill his lungs with air for him then and there! But the doctor's prescription would be daily breathing exercises, by which he would himself learn to take in more air, and thus gradually to increase his capacity for intake, and so enlarge 'the fulness' of which his lungs are capable when he breathes. Something similar applies to the Christian's experience of the fulness of the Holy Spirit. The extent to which the Spirit actually penetrates and possesses every moment of our time, every corner of our lives, and every sphere of our thought and activity, is always capable of enlargement. The Prayer Book Confirmation Service aptly and wisely prays for the candidate 'that he may ... *daily increase* in Thy Holy Spirit more and more'.

### TEMPORARY AND PERMANENT

At this point two important distinctions must be drawn.

The first is that between *temporary, occasional, and individual* manifestations of the Spirit's presence and those consequences of the Spirit's indwelling which are, or should be, *universal, permanent, and sustained.*

The difference here in mind is like the difference between the blossom and the fruit on a cherry tree. The appearance of blossom is a sign of life, and a promise of fruit. But it is a passing manifestation, a means to an end, not an end in itself. The true end of the life processes in the tree is the production of fruit. Fruit takes longer to mature, and is not so impressive to look at as blossom. Yet without it the tree must ultimately be classed as unproductive.

Similarly in the Church's experience of life in the Spirit God may sometimes in the early stages grant notable and comparatively sensational manifestations of His presence. So in the first days of the Christian Church, as we have already noticed, signs and wonders were wrought, the sick were healed and even the dead raised; and in not a few cases individuals who received the Spirit immediately began to speak in an abnormal fashion, in 'tongues'. At that initial stage in the Church's founding these special signs served effectively to confirm the faith and inform the conviction of the first believers. They were helped by such evidence to appreciate the reality and the range—reaching Samaritans and Gentiles, as well as Jews—of the salvation now given to all who put faith in Jesus as the crucified and exalted Christ. Comparable manifestations have from time to time appeared in the life of young churches on mission fields, and striking evidences of God's presence with them, and power in them, seem often to be given to young converts in a way which does not continue to the same extent when they are more established and mature. God, we may say, takes special pains in these cases to get His children off to a good start, and it is in these terms that the phenomena in question should be understood.

### 'YOU WILL KNOW THEM BY THEIR FRUITS'

But abnormal phenomena are as ambiguous as they are fascinating. As Jesus Himself taught, it is 'by their fruits', and not by signs and wonders, that the genuine are to be distinguished from the false. 'On that day', Jesus said, 'many will say to me, "Lord, Lord, did we not prophesy in your name, and cast out demons in your name, and do many mighty works in your name?" And then will I declare to them, "I never knew you; depart from me, you evildoers"' (see Mt. 7: 15-23).

Signs and wonders, though accompanying Christian profession, do not prove even that the agent is born again. We must remember that the phenomena of healings, visions, 'voices', prophetic utterance, and 'glossolalia'—speaking in unintelligible sounds—have all appeared from time to time in pagan and non-religious contexts, where they admit only of psychological, psychosomatic, or demonic explanation. It is not impossible that some instances of these phenomena within the Christian Church ought to be explained in the same terms.

The ultimate purpose of Christ's gift to His people of the indwelling Spirit was, and still is, to produce in their lives the fruit of Christlike living. This 'fruit of the Spirit' (cf. Gal. 5: 22f.) is both God's permanent requirement of all His children and His own distinctive product in them. The authentic mark of being 'filled with the Spirit' is that this fruit is appearing in us ever more prolifically. The decisive test is not the experiential but the ethical one.

### 'PUT LOVE FIRST'[1]

When Paul seeks to analyze 'the fruit of the Spirit' in Galatians 5: 22, the first element he names is love. When he seeks to raise the Corinthians' mind above their unhealthy and vainglorious preoccupation with specific manifestations like speaking in tongues, he points them to a 'more excellent way' —'the best way of all', as N.E.B. renders it—and this way is love. 'If I speak in the tongues of men and of angels, but have not love, I am a noisy gong or a clanging cymbal' (I Cor. 13: 1). 'Spiritual' activity is null and void where love is absent. This

[1] I Cor. 14: 1, N.E.B.

leads us to our second distinction, namely, that between the *fruit* of the Spirit, which is exhibited in the grace and gentleness of Christlike living, and the *gifts* which the Spirit gives to be exercised in ministry to our Christian brethren.

What are gifts? They are the equipment Christ bestows for the exercise of that mutual ministry and service which is the divinely prescribed pattern for congregational life. They are to be used, not for self-display, but 'for edification'—that is, the 'building up' of each other in Christian fellowship, whereby we lead each other on into fuller Christian maturity. In I Corinthians 12: 7, Paul calls gifts 'the manifestation of the Spirit', implying not only their divine origin, but also that through their use the Spirit-controlled life of God's people is made evident both to themselves and to others. But what, essentially, are they? To be specific: is there a common formula for such varied abilities and activities as are covered in I Corinthians 12: 28-30—'God has appointed in the church ... apostles ... prophets ... teachers ... workers of miracles ... healers, helpers, administrators, speakers in various kinds of tongues'? Yes, there is. It is this: a spiritual gift is *an ability to express and communicate in some way one's knowledge of Christ and His grace*. It is not a mere natural endowment, though usually it is given through the sanctifying of a natural endowment. Spiritual gifts communicate a spiritual content: they display the riches of Christ, by manifestation of something received from Him. Preaching, healing, working miracles, giving a helping hand, managing affairs, or speaking in tongues —all these activities display in some fashion both the nature and the power of the Christian salvation, and as such are to be seen as gifts of Christ Himself, given for the welfare of His Church. We ought however to recognize that the apostles were a unique order which cannot be repeated; and that prophets in the special sense of men given fresh revelation from God, of a kind necessary in the early Church until the New Testament was completed, are no longer necessary.

## THE BEST GIFTS

Gifts vary in value, according to whether they give more or less Christian help, at whatever level, to others. Thus, for example, speaking the Word of God in intelligible language is in this sense 'better' than speaking it in a tongue, for it does more good. 'Earnestly desire the *higher* gifts', says Paul (I Cor. 12: 31). Which are best? Clearly the best of all are gifts that issue in ministry of the Word: wisdom, knowledge, prophecy (i.e., the capacity to transmit messages from God whether received by immediate revelation or by reflection on the Scriptures), and, in general, all forms of the power to teach and apply divine truth. These are the gifts which made apostles, and which in our day make preachers, evangelists, and pastors. But the list in I Corinthians 12, as we saw, mentions other gifts, fitting men for other forms of service: extraordinary gifts like healing and miracles, more ordinary ones like the abilities of 'helpers' (the Greek word suggests the idea of 'taking over') and 'administrators'. These gifts, though comparatively unspectacular, are as necessary for the Church's life as is preaching. So are many more forms of service not listed here (for there is no reason to regard the list in I Corinthians 12: 28-30 as exhaustive).

In Romans 12: 6ff., another key passage on spiritual gifts, Paul's charge to his readers to use their God-given abilities starts, as we would expect, with the ministry of the Word, but it soon broadens (vv. 8ff.), without any sense of a change of subject, into a general plea for the exercise towards each other of the various graces of Christian character—showing mercy, kindness, consideration, hospitality, sympathy, and so on. Hereby it is made apparent that to show these qualities in serving others is to enjoy the privilege of exercising a spiritual gift no less really than a clergyman does when he preaches. This is a most important truth. No doubt 'gifts' and 'graces' are distinct in idea, but in practice much of our use of the former is simply a matter of giving appropriate exercise to the latter, informally and spontaneously, in seeking to meet human need in whatever form it confronts us. In other words, Good Samaritanship is as truly an employment of a spiritual gift as is good preaching.

Now it is right, and indeed obligatory, to 'desire the spiritual gifts' (I Cor. 14: 1), and to wish to see in congregational life the fulfilment of the apostle Peter's precept—'as each has received a gift, employ it for one another, as good stewards of God's varied grace' (I Pet. 4: 10). This is a sphere of great neglect in our churches. We acquiesce in a general lay passivity. To many churchmen the idea that they should be making some positive contribution to congregational life, over and above their modicum of financial help, still makes no appeal. We have a long way to go before we can know the full life of the Spirit at local congregational level. From this standpoint the present re-awakening of interest in spiritual gifts, and the growing concern that every Christian should have encouragement and freedom to use his gift in the church's corporate life (for none is wholly without gifts: see Rom. 12: 6; I Cor. 12: 7; Eph. 4: 7, 16), is something heartily to be welcomed. But we must beware of thinking too narrowly here. There is more than one sort of gift. There are the gifts of doing things to help people, as well as of helping them by talking to them. And among the gifts of utterance Paul is clear that 'prophecy', being intelligible, is preferable to 'tongues', which are not. 'I would rather speak five words with my mind, in order to instruct others, than ten thousand words in a tongue' (I Cor. 14: 19). So that if we equated 'gifts' with 'tongues', and assumed that any advance towards the New Testament ideal of universal mutual ministry in the local church was necessarily bound up with an extended practice of glossolalia, we should go completely astray.

It is no part of our purpose, when we say this, to pass a verdict on the charismatic movements of our time, nor to query the testimony of those who tell us that with glossolalia they have found spiritual release and advance. All we wish to do is to ensure that in thinking about these matters we do not lose our sense of proportion, or our awareness of the relative importance of things. Just at this point we are all in danger. We do not question the real importance of the blessings accompanying the practice of glossolalia for those who have personally received them; but we do question whether glossolalia in itself is of any major value for the Christian Church, one way or the other; and therefore we question very seriously whether those, on the one hand, who think it important to try to spread this practice, and those, on the other hand, who think it important to try to stamp it out, are not both showing a faulty sense of proportion. What is important is not that we either should or should not speak in tongues, but that, first, we should covet the best gifts rather than the second-best, and that, second, we should recognize that the true use of gifts is bound up, not with self-display, party spirit, or any 'holier-than-thou' complex, but with self-effacing, loving service of others for our Saviour's sake.

What has all this to do with our being filled with the Spirit? A great deal. In the first place, our argument shows that there is no necessary link between being filled with the Spirit and receiving the gift of tongues, nor yet—and this is important—the other way round! Secondly, it shows us that the question whether, or (better) how far, we are filled with the Spirit must finally be answered by reference, not to past experiences nor to present states of mind nor to particular manifestations, but to our character and behaviour in ordinary daily life. How far are we filled—that is, controlled and dominated—by the Spirit? This is the same as asking, How far are we occupying ourselves with the things that occupy the Spirit, and co-operating with Him in the task which He has been set within us to do? The Spirit is given to us, not to call attention to Himself, but to glorify the Lord Jesus Christ, both by revealing His glory to our hearts and by producing in our lives the fruit of increasing Christlikeness. Paul highlights both aspects of the Spirit's work when he describes the Christian life as follows: 'we all, with unveiled face, *beholding the glory of the Lord*, are being *changed into his likeness* from one degree of glory to another; for *this comes from the Lord who is the Spirit*' (II Cor. 3: 18).

How far then are we filled with the Spirit? The answer is: to the precise extent to which we want, and allow, the Spirit who indwells us to carry forward day by day His work of causing us to resemble our Lord.

CHAPTER EIGHT

# THE FELLOWSHIP OF THE CHURCH

Our task now is to develop the thought with which the last chapter but one closed.

In the Christian creeds, confession of faith in the Holy Spirit is directly followed by mention of the one, holy, catholic and apostolic Church, and the communion (that is, *fellowship*) of saints. This is right; for it is by the gift of the Spirit that the new community has been created, and that individuals are now baptized into vital membership in this one body (I Cor. 12: 13). So the day of Pentecost, with its outpouring of the Spirit by the ascended Lord on the gathered company of His disciples, has been aptly called the birthday of the Church.

In the Prayer Book Catechism the account of what one chiefly learns from the statements of the Creed includes this: 'I learn to believe ... in God the Holy Ghost, who sanctifieth me, and all the elect people of God'. Here attention is rightly called to the important truth that what the Spirit does for the individual believer He does for him not as a person being granted a private experience which has nothing to do with anyone else, but as one who is made a member of the Church of God. The blessing which thus becomes his is one that he shares with the whole company of God's believing people. It is this blessing indeed which initiates him into the reality of the communion of saints. It makes him a living member of the one body; and the new life to which he is now called is a life to be lived not in isolation but in fellowship. Fellowship (*koinonia* in the Greek) means, first, joint participation in something, and, second, sharing what you have with someone else. The two meanings, both related to Christ, together give us the biblical conception of the Church's life. It is a life, first and basically, of joint participation in Christ and His grace, and then, second and consequently, of sharing with our fellow-Christians all that Christ has given us individually.

### THE FELLOWSHIP OF THE HOLY SPIRIT

St. Paul finishes his second letter to the Corinthians with the familiar words: 'The grace of the Lord Jesus Christ and the love of God and the fellowship of the Holy Spirit be with you all' (II Cor. 13: 14; see R.S.V. mg.). These words emphasize that in the Gospel Christ meets us with grace, the Father deals with us in love, and the Spirit enriches us with His 'fellowship'; that is, with a 'participation in' His indwelling presence, which makes us one with God, and one with all who similarly participate in the one Spirit. So all true Christians share a common life, the life of the Spirit Himself; and we share it together in one body. In consequence, our prime responsibility is not to seek to create between Christians a unity which does not already exist, but to preserve and to express more openly and fully 'the unity of the Spirit' (see Eph. 4: 3) which is God-given, and into which by the one Spirit we have all been brought.

This truth concerning the divinely created unity of all Christians is one which many in our churches, and not least our own chief ministers, need to see, to believe, and to act on. It is plainly unchristian to insist, as many are doing, that Christians can lawfully come together at the Lord's Table only when they all accept and possess the ministry of episcopally ordained clergymen. The ministry and the sacrament alike are meant to serve the expression of our God-given unity in the Spirit with all who are Christ's, not to hinder that expression by being linked with a non-scriptural principle of this kind.

It is not our relation to the bishop of the diocese, nor our communion with the Archbishop of Canterbury, or with any other human 'head' (so-called) of the Church that entitles us to regard ourselves as one with other Christians and to meet with them at the Lord's Table, but our common relation to the one Lord and only Saviour, and our consequent fellowship or common participation in the one Spirit. Would that we heard less of the former and more of the latter!

This does not mean, of course, that the local church should not exercise discipline over professing Christians who are openly living in sin. As our Communion Service in the Book of Common Prayer rightly emphasizes, free access to the Lord's Table is only for those who truly repent and are in love and charity with their neighbours.

In what is said above about inter-communion we have in mind only Christians who are in good standing in their own churches.

### ALL SONS OF GOD

In Christ and through the Gospel all who believe are alike introduced into the same benefits. 'For there is', Paul writes, 'no distinction between Jew and Greek; the same Lord is Lord of all and bestows his riches upon all who call upon him' (Rom. 10: 12). The indwelling Spirit, given to all alike, makes us God's children, and marks us as such in His sight. 'Because you are sons', Paul writes, 'God has sent the Spirit of His Son into our hearts' (Gal. 4: 6).

Our common possession as God's children of the same Spirit of sonship marks us all as brethren of equal standing in God's family. It is, says Paul, through Christ, and 'in one Spirit', that Jew and Gentile both have access to the Father (Eph. 2: 18). Before Christ came, and before the Spirit was thus given, Jew and Gentile were radically separated, and in relation to God one was treated as 'near' and the other as 'far off'. But now in Christ and by the Spirit both have the same privilege of full access and both enjoy the same status of full sonship.

On this basis the Gospel is meant to unite in mutual love and fellowship types and classes of men which are naturally separated, with no prospects of unity or of living happily together. In local churches there is a widespread tendency to segregate groups which naturally cohere, like adolescents or young wives. But this is to make the Church look like the world! We do not say that youth fellowships or young wives' groups ought not to exist; but we do say that in every local church there should be deliberate concern to have groups meeting regularly whose membership evidences great variety. For God's distinctive grace is most clearly exhibited before men by the harmonious meeting and living together in intimate fellowship of a group or church whose members markedly differ in age and education, in race and colour, in culture and social standing, in work and natural interest; yet are 'all one in Christ Jesus' (Gal. 3: 28).

### GREAT DIVERSITY OF GIFT AND FUNCTION

Among Christians thus enjoying a common life in the Spirit there should normally emerge marked differences of individual gifts and functions, leading to a complex pattern of mutual interdependence.

Paul uses the body metaphor to make this truth plain. While by the one Spirit we are all equally baptized into the one body, yet as members of the body we each have our own distinct character and function. (See Rom. 12: 4f.; I Cor. 12: 12ff.) Spiritual gifts, as we saw earlier, are given in great variety, their character depending in each case upon the determination of the donor. The same Spirit, says Paul, apportions to each one individually as He wills (I Cor. 12: 4-7, 11). 'In each of us', he affirms, 'the Spirit is manifested in one particular way, for some useful purpose' (I Cor. 12: 7, N.E.B.). So Peter writes: 'Whatever gift each of you may have received, use it in service to one another, like good stewards dispensing the grace of God in its varied forms' (I Pet. 4: 10, N.E.B.).

Every Christian therefore should expect—and should be taught to expect—to have to discharge a stewardship in the exercise of some God-given gift in a divinely appointed form of service. This means that every congregation, and particularly those responsible for ordering the activities of the congregation, ought to realize that real scope and genuine encouragement must constantly be given for the gifts of the Spirit possessed by individuals to be discovered and developed, and thus increasingly exercised in ministry for the benefit and edification of all.

As things are in our churches, the scope usually given at this point is far too limited. We need to grasp afresh the scriptural conception of the local congregation as, so to speak, a team in which everyone has his own 'game' to play. The conventional picture of the local church as a company of people who spend their time together merely as an audience, or as spectators, while the same one or two men fulfil all the ministries on every occasion, is a travesty of the New Testament view.

How then should our inherited patterns of local church life be remodelled, so that the New Testament view may find fuller expression? The question is far-reaching, and our danger is not to think it through radically enough.

Some, for instance, will say at once that the great need is for the speaking in church (i.e., the public praying and preaching) to be shared round among more members of the congregation. Others call for more free extempore prayer in public worship. Others speak as if the vital thing is to reintroduce charismatic 'prophecy' (relaying unpremeditated messages from God) and tongues (interpreted, of course: see I Cor. 14: 27f.) into church meetings. On all these suggestions, we have just two comments to make.

The first is that they are *serious* suggestions, and must be treated as such. To dismiss them on the grounds that the things envisaged would be unconventional, or socially lowering, or in some other way 'not quite nice', would be mere worldliness. To recoil from them as 'un-Anglican activities', saying in effect, to quote the old song:

> Oh—you can't do that there 'ere;
> No—you can't do that there 'ere;
> Anywhere else you could do that there,
> But you can't do that there 'ere!

would be to show all the symptoms of sectarianism and church-pride. If we reject these suggestions, it must only be after sympathetic consideration, and on a thought-out basis of scriptural principle, not on an unreflective snap judgment born of nothing more creditable than ecclesiastical or cultural prejudice. Whether the proposed changes are likely to issue in an increased edification for the congregation as a whole is indeed a question which might have to be answered differently from place to place. Certainly in every place it is desirable to be governed by the principle that 'all things should be done decently and in order' (1 Cor. 14: 40). But we shall not attempt to discuss such matters here. It is on our second comment that we want to lay our stress.

For the second comment is that, whatever value these suggestions may be thought to have in themselves, as answers to the question of how our church life should be remodelled they are *inadequate*. They operate within the institutionalized, formalized thought-world which defines church life in terms of a sequence of 'meetings'—no less, no more. But our first need is to break away from this over-narrow conception. For the New Testament ideal of the local church is of a company of people bound together in a fellowship of constant ministry to the needs of each other and of all men, needs both spiritual and physical—needs, in fact, at every level of life. The thought of 'spiritual gifts' is therefore foreshortened if we limit it to vocal powers for use in 'meetings'. In the passage referred to earlier, where Peter urges 'whatever gift each of you may have received, use it in service to one another', it is noticeable that he goes on to illustrate his meaning, not simply with reference to speaking ('whoever *speaks*, as one who utters oracles of God'), but with reference also to Good Samaritanship in the widest sense ('whoever *renders service*, as one who renders it by the strength which God supplies'). The word translated 'render service' is the regular word for 'minister'. (See I Pet. 4: 10, 11.)

A 'gift', therefore, as we have seen already, is essentially a capacity to render service; and there will be as many kinds of 'gifts' as there are forms of service to be rendered. So a doctrine of 'gifts' which centred entirely on powers of utterance and instruction, and laid no stress, for instance, on giving money, being helpful, showing sympathy (see Rom. 12: 8, 15), visiting and relieving those in need (see Jas. 1: 27; Mat. 25: 37-39), and managing affairs (I Cor. 12: 28), would be disastrously narrow, as would be the idea of church life that went with it. And such a doctrine would tend to quench the Spirit; for it would obscure the fact that it is by assiduously using this less spectacular class of gifts, necessarily out of 'meeting' time, that many Christians are intended to make their major contribution to the local church's life.

But having said that, we must insist that provision should everywhere be made for all members of each local church to become vocal at some point in the fellowship of testimony, exhortation, and prayer. This will not, in all probability, be best done in the Sunday services but rather in informal small gatherings during the week, which will form part of the rhythm of every healthy local church's life. For this purpose big congregations must be broken down into cross-sectional groups small enough for everyone in them to take part, and to give as well as receive. Local situations will prescribe their own detailed pattern; but in some form or other this kind of fellowship must take place if the full range of the Spirit's gifts to the members of Christ is to be appreciated and used.

NEW EXPRESSIONS OF EPISCOPAL OVERSIGHT

When Paul addressed the elders (presbyters) of the church at Ephesus he said to them, 'Take heed unto yourselves, and to all the flock, in the which the Holy Ghost hath made you *bishops*, to feed the church of God' (Acts 20: 28 R.V.; the word rendered 'bishops' is *episkopous*). Those whom the Holy Spirit is here said to have appointed as bishops—that is, 'overseers'—were a group of men in a single local church. If this work of oversight, or 'episcopacy', was one of caring for the flock, and watching as a shepherd over the needs of individual sheep, it is understandable that several would be needed adequately to shepherd a large congregation. This is a far cry from diocesan episcopacy as we now know it in the Anglican Communion, in which it is impossible for the one bishop to care for every person in his diocese.

We need to regain from the New Testament a new awareness of what episcopal oversight is, and how it should be discharged. For even when we recognize that it is the vicar of a parish, rather than his diocesan, who is the present-day equivalent of the elders of the church at Ephesus, it still remains subscriptural for the spiritual care of a large congregation to be the responsibility of one man. Pastoral overloading and inadequate shepherding are the inevitable result. Several ought to share in the oversight together. Nor were New Testament elders imported from elsewhere, as a new vicar is today. They were all found from within the particular local congregation. The equivalent in our day would be for men who at present serve as lay readers or churchwardens to share fully in the pastoral responsibility which our present system assigns to the incumbent. One longs to see incumbents who, recognizing that this is what the New Testament pattern requires, will make this venture in faith, believing that God will grant to individuals the necessary gifts which by experience will reach mature development.

It is interesting in this connection to notice the words of the writer to the Hebrews: 'See to it that no one fail to obtain the grace of God; that no "root of bitterness" spring up and cause trouble, and by it the many become defiled' (Heb. 12: 15). For the Greek word used for 'see to it' means literally 'to exercise oversight' or 'to function as a bishop'; and here it is in the plural, addressed as a command to the whole congregation. So here, instead of one bishop overseeing the many, the many are told to exercise oversight of each other. This confirms our point, adumbrated earlier, that we need in our churches a new sense of responsibility for mutual spiritual care (see Gal. 6: 1).

## TELL IT TO THE CHURCH

It is noteworthy also that, when (see Mat. 18: 15ff.) our Lord spoke of two brethren at variance, needing to be reconciled and unable to come to agreement, He taught that the next step ought to be for the matter to be referred to two or three other brethren (that is, ordinary church members). This implies the same truth: all church members should share together the responsibilities of spiritual care for one another.

Our Lord went on to say that if what the two or three say does not prove decisive, the matter should be told to the 'church'. This cannot mean to a single presiding minister. It must mean to a representative church meeting, in which a number together seek before God to come in the Spirit to a responsible Christian attitude; and then to give appropriate advice, and take appropriate action. Here, too, is something which we urgently need to practise if the Spirit's ministry is to be fully experienced and enjoyed in our churches today.

### THE FUNCTION OF FULL-TIME MINISTERS

This does not mean, of course, that there is no place or need for special, full-time 'ordained' ministers. But we need to rethink their functions. Their personal shepherd-relation to the flock is fundamental and must not under any circumstances be weakened. But it is not proper that all the ministry and local oversight should be permanently left in their hands. Their task should rather be understood as to teach and train, guide and encourage, the church members themselves increasingly to engage in ministry, pastoral care, and oversight of each other. This is indicated by St. Paul in his letter to the Ephesians. There he says that the ascended Lord gave 'some to be apostles, some prophets, some evangelists, some pastors and teachers' not to do all the work themselves, but 'to *equip God's people for work in his service* to the building up of the body of Christ' (Eph. 4: 11-12, N.E.B.). Only as all fulfil their different ministries will the body of Christ be built up as God intends that it should.

CHAPTER NINE

# THE LEADING OF THE SPIRIT

The gift of the indwelling Spirit is particularly associated in the teaching of our Lord and the records of the New Testament with the promise and experience of guidance in the way to go, in both our thoughts and actions. Jesus told the apostles, 'When the Spirit of truth comes, *he will guide you* into all the truth' (Jn. 16: 13). Writing to the Christians in Rome, Paul declares, 'For all who are *led by the Spirit of God*' [led, that is, to fight and mortify sin; see the context] 'are sons of God' (Rom. 8: 14). The decision of the Church Council at Jerusalem included the words: 'It has seemed good *to the Holy Spirit and to us*' (Acts 15: 28). Awareness of the Spirit's leading as these texts characterize it seems widely lacking in our day. It is not sought, nor expected, nor do we know how to recognize it. For this reason we urgently need to enquire how the guidance of the Spirit may be more fully experienced in the life both of individual Christians and of the corporate fellowship of God's people.

### GUIDANCE INTO ALL TRUTH

The primary work of the Spirit, as we have seen, is to glorify Jesus Christ, and to lead willing learners into the discovery and understanding of all the truth concerning Christ's person and work; for this is the very heart of the Gospel and of Christian faith.

Such guidance was first given by the Spirit to the apostles, who had companied with Jesus and heard His teaching, and who lived through the great events of His passion and resurrection and the manifestation of the Spirit in the early days of the Church. Christ's promise to them was: 'When the Spirit of truth comes, he will guide you into all the truth'; 'he will take what is mine and declare it to you'; 'he will teach you all things, and bring to your remembrance all that I have said to you' (Jn. 16: 13, 15; 14: 26). Their destiny, as eyewitnesses of these events, was to become the authoritative reporters and interpreters of Christ for all time, so that in every generation it would be 'through their word' (Jn. 17: 20) that others would believe. The fulfilment of this promise (for it *was* fulfilled!) means that the apostles became, not merely the *first* believers, but also the *standard* believers, by whose beliefs all who came after them must measure and reform their own. The understanding to which the apostles were brought by this guidance is permanently recorded in the writings of the New Testament.

Not that the new Testament writings ever stood, or could stand, alone. They themselves show how deeply the minds of the apostolic writers were soaked in the Scriptures of the Old Testament, which they regarded as themselves the words of the Holy Spirit (see Acts 1: 16; 4: 25; 28: 25; Heb. 3: 7; 9: 8; 10: 15; II Pet. 1: 21), pointing to Christ (see Acts 3: 18, 21-24; I Pet. 1: 10-12), written indeed chiefly for Christians (see Rom. 15: 4; I Cor. 10: 11; II Tim. 3: 16), and yielding their full saving message only to those who learn to read them in the light of Christ (see II Cor. 3: 14-16; II Tim. 3: 15). In this they were, of course, simply reproducing what Christ Himself had taught them (see Mt. 5: 17-20; Jn. 5: 39; Lk. 24: 25-27, 32, 44-47). It is clear that from the start they took for granted the status of the Old Testament as Christian Scripture, and taught Gentiles as well as Jews so to regard it. From the first, the Old Testament Scriptures and the apostolic sermons and writings were understood to belong together, as complementary parts of a single divine revelation. It is to this understanding that later generations have borne witness by binding up the two sets of books within one pair of covers and calling the resulting volume, not 'A library of Jewish and Christian classics', or any such title, but 'The Holy Bible'—a single book, written in two parts over more than a thousand years by a very varied group of authors, but telling a single story and carrying a single message, namely the good news of Jesus Christ.

If we today are to profit from the guidance of the Spirit in matters of faith, and thus be led into a right understanding of Christian truth, it is these Scriptures which we must study. Just as a human teacher has a right to choose what text-book he will use, and, when he has himself written a text-book, will naturally prefer to use that, so it is with the Holy Spirit: the basic text from which He teaches is Holy Scripture, and nothing that is not in direct and demonstrable accord with Scripture can be regarded as taught by Him.

Teaching of individuals by God Himself was promised in Old Testament times. As Jesus said, 'It is written in the prophets, "And they shall all be taught of God" ' (Jn. 6: 45, cf. Is. 54: 13). Evidently Jesus understood this of the Spirit's distinctive work as the Father's emissary pointing men to the Son, for He went straight on to say: 'Every one who has heard and learned from the Father comes to me'. Paul says to the Christians in Thessalonica: 'You yourselves have been taught by God' (I Thess. 4: 9). Similarly St. John in his first letter declares, 'But you have been anointed by the Holy One, and you all know [have knowledge]'. 'The anointing which you received from him abides in you, and you have no need that any one should teach you; as his anointing teaches you about everything, and is true, and is no lie' (I Jn. 2: 20, 27).

In this sphere every disciple of Christ should experience for himself the direct personal guidance and illumination of the Spirit. The condition of finding is simply to seek, by humble, prayerful, expectant attention to the Scriptures as we hear and read them. Once this experience is tasted, the individual will gain a new delight in studying and dwelling on God's Word. But are individuals in our churches being encouraged, as they ought to be, to believe that if they will seriously and prayerfully give themselves to Bible study, God the Spirit will be their teacher and guide? Much may be said, and needs to be said, about the danger of fanciful and frivolous individualism in Bible study, and the importance of recognizing that it is only 'with all the saints' (Eph. 3: 18)—that is, in fellowship with other Christians, and through benefitting from the gifts of those whom God has equipped to be teachers in the Church—that spiritual understanding normally makes healthy advance. Nevertheless granted all that, it is a grim sign of how far we have fallen when Protestants are found reverting to the old Roman view (which Rome has now professedly abandoned!) that Bible reading is too risky to be rewarding for lay people, and that to treat it as an important means of grace is therefore a mistake. This point of view—not, unfortunately, uncommon at the present time—bears melancholy witness to our loss of faith in the promised ministry of the Holy Spirit.

KNOWING HOW TO PRAY

It is also the work of the indwelling Spirit to lead us to seek God's face, to experience free and full access to His presence, to make known our requests, and, above all, to intercede for the doing of God's will and the coming of His kingdom. In this ministry of intercession we naturally lack both zeal and understanding. 'We do not know how to pray as we ought.' But just here 'the Spirit helps us in our weakness'. For by His presence within He can sustain and guide our praying, and beyond what can be fully expressed in words He will intercede 'for us' and 'for the saints', 'according to the will of God'. (See Rom. 8: 26f.)

The historic evangelical insistence that private prayer should be free and spontaneous rather than a routine of set forms ('saying prayers') reflects strong faith in the effectiveness of this aspect of the Spirit's ministry. Do we retain this faith today? How much do we know in experience of the Spirit's leading in intercession, and of His own interceding activity? All too little, one fears.

CONSTRAINT TO PREACH CHRIST

A further reason why the Spirit has been given to indwell Christ's followers is to ensure that witness to Christ and the Gospel is given 'to all nations, beginning from Jerusalem' (see Lk. 24: 45-49; Acts 1: 8). So in the Acts of the Apostles we find that the prime mover in the sustained witness and increasing outreach of the early evangelism was the Spirit Himself. He gave boldness of utterance in testimony which amazed the hearers (see Acts 4: 13, 31). When Stephen preached in Jerusalem many disputed with him, but 'they could not withstand the wisdom and the Spirit with which he spoke' (Acts 6: 10).

So, too, it was the Spirit who directed Philip to go and join the chariot of a passing foreigner, an Ethiopian whom Philip found to be an eager seeker and enquirer (see Acts 8: 26ff.). It was the Spirit who compelled Peter, against all his inherited practice and prejudice, to go to the house of Cornelius to make the Gospel known (see Acts 10: 9–23). When taken to task in Jerusalem concerning his behaviour Peter was able to testify that 'the Spirit told me to go with them making no distinction' (Acts 11: 12).

How little we seem to know today in our churches and in our personal lives of this divine urge to evangelism; of this guidance of the Spirit to go, quite contrary maybe to our own expectation or natural choice, and of this experience of finding prepared souls who are only waiting for someone to preach to them Jesus and to lead them to personal faith in Him. Maybe the crucial question to ask is, Are we willing to be constrained? Are we ready to recognize and respond to the Spirit's compulsion in this matter?

### CALLED TO SPECIAL MINISTRY

When God's time came for the Gospel to be spread beyond Palestine, and for existing congregations to promote this missionary and evangelistic enterprise, it was the Spirit who both constrained Paul and Barnabas to go, and made the local church members at Antioch aware that it was their privilege and responsibility to send them (see Acts 13: 1–4).

It is right and proper that in the initial ordination of a man to the ministry (i.e., in the Church of England, to the diaconate) the first question which he is asked is, 'Do you trust that you are inwardly moved by the Holy Ghost to take upon you this office and ministration, to serve God for the promoting of his glory, and the edifying of his people?' To verify the initiative and call of the Spirit must always be the Church's first step when setting men apart for any particular sphere of ministry; for without it, candidates would fall under the same condemnation as those of whom God said: 'I did not send the prophets, yet they ran' (Jer. 23: 21).

It is important also that the congregations from which such candidates come, or to which by personal contact they have become known, should also feel the constraint of the Spirit to share in separating them to their divinely-appointed task, in commending them to the grace of God, and in supporting them by active practical interest. They should also, by testimony to the candidate's gifts and character be able to confirm his own personal conviction that he is called of God to this ministry; for if God has not equipped a man for a job, then He has not in reality called him to it, whatever the man may imagine. Some congregations need to start further back and to begin to pray God by His Spirit to separate and send forth some from their midst to the work of the Gospel. A local church that produces no labourers to send forth into God's harvest field is in no good case.

### DIRECTION TO RIGHT SPHERES OF SERVICE

Those called to leave their home church or previous occupation and to devote their entire lives to Christian ministry, particularly need guidance concerning right spheres of service. Here too God's Spirit can and should be trusted to guide.

Sometimes the Spirit calls a man to a task by confronting him with a work waiting to be done, and by making him aware that he is the person to undertake it. Barnabas and Saul were in this way definitely called and sent by the Spirit to the work which they were to fulfil.

At other times, when Christian workers are already active in one sphere, the Spirit may begin to guide concerning their next sphere by firmly and unmistakably closing or keeping shut doors of opportunity which it seemed attractive or obvious to attempt to enter next. So Paul and Silas, having gone through Syria and Cilicia, Phrygia and Galatia strengthening the churches, were 'forbidden by the Holy Spirit to speak the word in Asia'. Then they 'attempted to go into Bithynia, but the Spirit of Jesus did not allow them'. Then, after accepting the guidance of God's 'No' twice repeated, they were given at Troas unmistakable, if unexpected, indication that God was now calling them to preach the Gospel in Macedonia. (See Acts 15: 40–16: 10.)

It is noteworthy that this guidance was given not to men who were sitting still waiting for God to move them, but to men who were both on the watch and on the move, actively fulfilling God's will as it had been made known to them thus far. We do not know all the circumstances and the means which the Spirit used on this occasion to make His mind plain. But we do know that Paul and Silas were conscious, as they sought to move on, not of frustrating limitation but rather of the satisfying freedom of divine control. The record is written for our instruction. Let us learn that for those who are on the move in God's service, and are genuinely willing to be guided of God concerning where next, similar experience of the restraint and constraint of the Spirit can be expected, so that they will not be left in uncertainty as to their Master's purpose for them.

### DECIDING ISSUES BY THE SPIRIT'S LEADING

At the Jerusalem Church Council (as recorded in Acts 15) a big question of Christian faith and practice had to be faced and settled. They had to decide whether those who taught that circumcision and observance of the Mosaic ritual law were essential to salvation in Christ were right or wrong. Clearly those present became very conscious of the leading of the Spirit—what was once described as 'the senior partnership of the Holy Ghost'. So it was that when they came to register a decision they realized that the Holy Spirit had already, so to speak, proposed the right course of action and that all they had to do was to second and support the motion. So they were able to say, 'It has seemed good to the Holy Spirit and to us' (Acts 15: 28).

How then did they discern the Spirit's leading so clearly? It seems to have happened through the contributions made to the discussion by the various speakers; in particular, Peter's testimony as to how, when he preached the Gospel to uncircumcised Gentiles in the house of Cornelius, they had been given the Holy Spirit by God without any precondition other than believing in Christ. This indication of the divine leading was further confirmed by the testimony of Barnabas and Paul concerning their missionary journey. They produced abundant evidence to show that God had opened a door of faith to the Gentiles.

These narratives were enough in themselves to create a strong presumption of the non-necessity of the Mosaic ordinances for Gentiles. But decisive guidance as to right and wrong in matters of theology must be drawn, not from events as such, however striking—for the book of providence, and Church history, is by no means self-interpreting—but from God's truth as set forth in the Bible. So Peter argued from the Gospel. How, he asked, could the law save Gentiles, when it had never saved a single Jew? It was 'a yoke... which neither our fathers nor we have been able to bear. But we believe that we shall be saved through the grace of the Lord Jesus, just as they will' (Acts 15: 10f.). And James found support for these (to Jews) unexpected developments in the Old Testament Scriptures, in prophecies which foretold the incoming of the Gentiles into the restored Kingdom of David (Acts 15: 16ff.).

From this we learn that we may expect the Spirit to guide us, and to help us to right decision, in our corporate counsels as well as our personal problems, by making us aware of His intervention and overruling in events that happen—often a number of seemingly independent events, coming together in a significant-seeming way—and by leading us to discern confirming interpretative teaching in the Scriptures themselves.

CHAPTER TEN

# ASSURANCE AND HOPE

God, unlike many men, is utterly straightforward, and wants people to know exactly where they stand with Him. He wants unbelievers to be quite clear that without Christ they are lost, and equally He intends believers to be out of doubt that in Christ they are both saved and safe.

## ETERNAL SECURITY

Objectively, the Christian's security rests on three grounds. The first is God's faithfulness to His *nature*. 'I the Lord do not change' (Mal. 3: 6). 'Jesus Christ is the same yesterday and today and for ever' (Heb. 13: 8). God, as Father, Son, and Spirit, never cease to be what He once was, and never acts out of character. What God is in the Bible He continues to be to all eternity. He appears in the Bible as an almighty Saviour, 'the God of all grace' (I Pet. 5: 10), and such He remains today.

The second ground of Christian security is God's faithfulness to His *Word*. 'God is not man, that he should lie, or a son of man, that he should repent' (Num. 23: 19). 'And now, O Lord, thou art God, and thy words are true, and thou hast promised...' (II Sam. 7: 28). God is, as David Livingstone put it, 'an honourable gentleman who never breaks His word'. God has promised that 'whoever calls on the name of the Lord *shall be saved*' (Acts 2: 21), and that promise will be kept. Jesus Christ has promised: 'My sheep hear my voice, and I know them, and they follow me; and *I give them eternal life, and they shall never perish, and no one shall snatch them out of my hand*' (Jn. 10: 27f.). This promise too will be kept. It is common in this connection to speak of the perseverance of the saints, but it would be better to speak of the *preservation* of the saints through the *perseverance* of the Saviour. He has promised to keep His own secure, and keep them He will. And in the same way all God's 'precious and very great promises' will find fulfilment (II Pet. 1: 4), for 'all the promises of God find their Yes in him [Jesus Christ]' (II Cor. 1: 20). Christian security is thus founded in the unchanging promises of an unchanging, promise-keeping God.

With this, as the third and final ground, goes God's faithfulness to His *work*. The plans which He has begun to put into execution will be completed. What He starts He finishes. If He loved us at the cross, He will love us for ever. 'He who did not spare his own Son but gave him up for us all, will he not also give us all things with him?' (Rom. 8: 32). 'Since, therefore, we are now justified by his blood, much more shall we be saved by him from the wrath of God. For if while we were enemies we were reconciled to God by the death of his Son, much more, now that we are reconciled, shall we be saved by his life' (Rom. 5: 9f.). Similarly if God has wrought in us new birth, and given us His Spirit to indwell us and progressively transform us into the Saviour's image, He will not abandon His work half-way and leave it unfinished. 'I am sure', wrote Paul to the Philippians, 'that he who began a good work in you will bring it to completion at the day of Jesus Christ' (Phil. 1: 6). Christians, writes Peter, 'by God's power are guarded through faith for a salvation ready to be revealed in the last time' (I Pet. 1: 5). The gift of the Spirit is itself a guarantee that the work of grace will be completed. 'If the Spirit of him who raised Jesus from the dead dwells in you, he who raised Christ Jesus from the dead will give life to your mortal bodies also through his Spirit which dwells in you' (Rom. 8: 11).

Objectively, therefore, it is certain that everyone who has repented and put faith in Jesus Christ as Saviour and Lord is saved, and safe, for all eternity. Well does the 'Revised Catechism' end by answering the question: 'What, then, is our assurance as Christians?' in the following terms: 'Our assurance as Christians is that neither death, nor life, nor things present, nor things to come, shall be able to separate us from the love of God, which is in Christ Jesus our Lord. Thus, daily increasing in God's Holy Spirit, and following the example of our Saviour Christ, we shall at the last be made like unto him, for we shall see him as he is' (Q.61: echoing Rom. 8: 38f. and I Jn. 3: 2).

GOD MEANS US TO BE SURE

But the objective security of the Christian in his present acceptance and prospect of bliss is not always subjectively realized. Many true Christians lack assurance concerning their relation to God and membership of His family. Some clergy appear to believe that no such full assurance is available, and that to think and say that one enjoys it is presumption, conceit, and self-deception. This state of affairs must however be regarded as both unhappy and unscriptural.

James Denney once observed that the touchstone of any version of Christianity is its doctrine of assurance, and he illustrated his meaning by saying that, whereas in conventional Catholicism assurance is a sin, and in conventional Protestantism it is a duty, in the New Testament assurance is simply a *fact*. He was right. The New Testament never discusses assurance as a topic, because lack of assurance was not in those days a problem. (The nearest thing to such a discussion is the first epistle of John, which was written partly to *re*assure Christians whose prior assurance had been shaken by false teachers telling them that they were really still in darkness; but this is a different issue from that of leading into assurance Christians who have never had it.) Throughout the New Testament it is taken for granted that Christians are joyfully certain of their standing in God's grace, their sonship in His family, and their hope of His glory—all the good things, in fact, which are spelled out in sequence as belonging to 'us' —Paul and all his Christian readers—in chapter 8 of the epistle to the Romans.

Whence came this certainty? From the ministry of the indwelling Spirit—that is, from the attitudes, convictions, and habits which He implanted. It was the Spirit who gave those first Christians confidence and liberty, and made it their deepest instinct, to call on God as 'Father'; and, writes Paul, 'When we cry "Abba! Father!" ['Abba' is simply the Aramaic for 'Father'] it is the Spirit himself bearing witness with our spirit that we are children of God' (Rom. 8: 15f.; see also Gal. 4: 6). Earlier in Romans he had written that the love of God, as shown forth at the cross, 'has been poured into our hearts through the Holy Spirit which has been given to us' (Rom. 5: 5). It was with reference to these new awarenesses and the habits that went with them, including the habit of not habitually sinning (see I Jn. 3: 9; 5: 18), that John declared: 'By this we know that he abides in us, by the Spirit which he has given us'; and again, 'By this we know that we abide in him and he in us, because he has given us of his own Spirit' (I Jn. 3: 24; 4: 13).

THE GUARANTEE OF OUR INHERITANCE

Moreover, the gift of the indwelling Spirit, of which Christians beome aware in the manner described by discovering the change that the Spirit has wrought in them, is intended to assure Christians of their future resurrection and glory with Christ, no less than of their present standing in grace through Christ. So, having written to the Corinthians about 'putting on our heavenly dwelling', in the day when 'that which is mortal' will be 'swallowed up by life', Paul added: 'He who has prepared us for this very thing is God, who has given us the Spirit as a guarantee' (see II Cor. 5: 1–5). The word translated 'guarantee' combines the thoughts of 'pledge', 'deposit on account', and 'first instalment'. It appears again in Ephesians 1: 13f., where Paul says that the Spirit, whom his readers have received as God's 'seal' (sign of ownership) set on them, 'is the guarantee of our inheritance until we acquire possession of it'. According, therefore, to New Testament teaching, as verified in the experience of New Testament Christians, the gift of the Spirit brings strong hope of eternal happiness, as well as confident certainty regarding one's present acceptance.

It thus appears that so far from the enjoyment of assurance

indicating that one is presumptuous, conceited, and self-deceived, the non-enjoyment of it proclaims an unhealthy and sub-normal spiritual condition. It appears too that those who oppose the teaching and decry the experience of assurance are themselves guilty of presumption and conceit, in their audacious preference for anti-scriptural doctrine.

Further still, it appears, too, that the Prayer Book Order for the Burial of the Dead is entirely right, by biblical standards, when it invites us to declare at the graveside of a departed believer: 'We therefore commit his body to the ground ... in sure and certain hope of the resurrection to eternal life, through our Lord Jesus Christ'. Prayers for the dead in Christ, asking that they may enjoy peace and bliss, are not only unnecessary, but out of place. They cannot be used without giving an impression of uncertainty, or contingency, about something which the New Testament sees as a certainty, guaranteed by the promise of God and the gift of His Spirit. Rather we should with solemn joy and in strong confidence thank God that the departed are 'with Christ', which is 'far better' (see Phil. 1:23), and that all that God has promised in Christ will now be theirs. The right way to commemorate the faithful departed is not by making petitions on their behalf, but by thanking God for them, and for His grace in their lives, and by letting their good example move us to seek more faithfulness in our own pilgrimage, so that 'with them we may be partakers' of God's 'heavenly kingdom'.

The widespread discontent with this, the Prayer Book attitude, and the reintroduction of prayers for the dead in so many recent Anglican liturgies, are melancholy signs of the weakness of our grasp of these things. If we understood better the meaning of the gift of the indwelling Spirit, it would be a different story. But this is just what many churchmen today do not understand. Hence the widespread lack, not merely of assurance but of interest in assurance, and the yawning gap between the Christian experience of the New Testament Church and what goes under the same name in churches today. Hence also the need to end this book, if it is to be of practical usefulness, by considering the question: How may we help into assurance churchmen who lack it?

### THE WAY OF ASSURANCE

In answering this question we must begin at the beginning. One has to be a Christian before one can know oneself to be a Christian, and one has to know the Gospel before one can be a Christian. So the first step is to make sure that the person we wish to help understands the meaning of sin, Christ's atoning death, repentance, and faith, and has personally sought to turn from a life of self-will to trust the living Christ as his Saviour and Master.

The second step is to make him aware of the reality of the Spirit's indwelling. Ways of doing this are by asking such questions as these:

Has Jesus Christ been glorified before the eyes of your spirit? Have you come to adore Him as your Lord and your God? Have you come to glory in the cross, and to see that your only hope lies in the fact that Jesus died for you? Has the thought that Jesus is alive taken hold of your mind, so that you know you can talk to Him and have fellowship with Him anywhere, and you know too that you go through life under His eye and in His company? Does your heart warm to the thought that He is on the throne of the universe, and will one day triumph visibly over all who now oppose Him? It is not nature but the indwelling Spirit that begets such a sense of the glory of Christ. (See Jn. 16: 14; I Cor. 12: 3.)

Have you come to see that when Christ bore the curse of the law on the cross, God was exposing both your sin and His love for you despite your sin? Do you recognize that His redeeming love for you was love for one who did not in the least deserve it, one who in fact deserved its opposite? Do you feel the constraint of Christ's love, the sheer impossibility of living any more in disregard of God now that you know you have been loved like that? Do you find yourself ashamed of the feebleness of your response to the love of the Father and the Son? It is not nature, but the indwelling Spirit, that is the source of this shedding abroad of the love of God in your heart. (See Rom. 5: 5.)

Have you a filial instinct prompting you to call God 'Father', and to trust and love Him as your Father, and to submit to His fatherly discipline when things go otherwise than you would have hoped? Do you actually talk to Him as a child to a father when you pray? Do you actually feel bound to obey Him in the way that children feel they ought to do what their parents say? (Not that they always do it, of course—but then, neither do you always obey God.) It is not from nature but from the indwelling Spirit that these filial impulses spring. (See Gal. 4: 6.)

Are you spiritually-minded? What are the things you want most of all? Is your ultimate target to know God, to see Him in action, to have His will done? Is it clear to you that this is the only thing that can ultimately satisfy your heart? What do you think about when you are not thinking about anything in particular? Does your mind at such times 'home' on God, and the things of God? Do you find the Bible absorbing because it shows you God? 'Those who live according to the flesh set their minds on the things of the flesh, but those who live according to the Spirit set their minds on the things of the Spirit' (Rom. 8: 5). If you are setting your mind on the things of the Spirit, it is the indwelling Spirit Himself who has brought it about.

Do you seek to walk by the Spirit, not fulfilling the lusts of the flesh? Are you conscious of inner conflict as the law of sin wars in your members, constantly distracting and diverting you from whole-hearted service of God? Only those who are indwelt by the Spirit ever experience such a conflict, for only they are set to serve God whole-heartedly in the first instance. Only they therefore find within themselves the state of affairs described by St. Paul: 'The desires of the flesh are against the Spirit, and the desires of the Spirit are against the flesh' (Gal. 5: 17). The more one yields as a Christian to the clamourings of sinful and self-indulgent impulse, and the more half-hearted one allows one's Christian living to become, the more one acts out of character, quenches and grieves the Spirit, and dishonours and displeases Christ (see Rev. 3: 15-19); and the less one acts like a Christian, the less can one expect to enjoy assurance that one is a Christian. But if you are seeking daily to 'make holiness perfect in the fear of God' (II Cor. 7: 1), your life is clear evidence that you have been born again, and are now indwelt, by the sovereign Holy Spirit.

What one is doing in asking such questions, of oneself and others, is to test the reality of professed repentance and faith, and at the same time to detect the evidence of the Spirit's present indwelling. By this means, spontaneously, those interrogated may come into the state described in Hebrews 10: 22 as 'full assurance of faith'—that state, that is, in which they find within themselves the certainty that Christ is theirs, and they are Christ's, for ever. False ideas, or at least the absence of true ones, coupled perhaps with inadequate Christian living, may have kept assurance out of their reach for a long time. But the New Testament shows that assurance (what the Reformers called *fiducia*, conscious confidence) is an integral element in normal healthy faith; and as Christians are made conscious, in the way New Testament Christians were conscious, of the Spirit's indwelling presence within them, so by His own power the Spirit is able to awaken within them a glowing conviction of their happiness and security as sons and heirs of God, leading them to 'rejoice with unutterable and exalted joy' (I Pet. 1: 8). Anyone who has seen how troubled faces light up as these things are explained and become clear will know what we mean.

In this connection it may be asked whether the scriptural way to understand the real nature of the liberating experience to which some in our day testify, giving it the name (incorrectly, as we saw) of 'baptism with (or, in) the Holy Spirit', is not to see it as a deepening, or intensification, of assurance. God is too good to withhold or withdraw His blessings because our ideas about them are wrong, and this would not be the first occasion on which He has blessed persons who have truly sought His face in ways which they did not themselves properly understand.

May God help us all truly to believe in, and faithfully to walk by, His indwelling Spirit! May God deepen His Spirit's ministry in all our hearts and lives!

'Now to him who *by the power at work within us* is able to do far more abundantly than all that we ask or think, to him be glory in the church and in Christ Jesus to all generations, for ever and ever, Amen' (Eph. 3: 20f.).

## Other Related Titles by Solid Ground Books

In addition to *The Spirit Within You* which you now hold in your hands, Solid Ground has also published the following classic books on the person and ministry of the Holy Spirit.

***THE PERSON AND WORK OF THE HOLY SPIRIT*** by B.B. Warfield
This precious book contains all the sermons, articles and book reviews on this vital subject by one of the most brilliant theologians America has ever produced. Sinclair Ferguson, author and pastor, said, "I commend these pages, as one who has continually been helped by their contents. It is a treasure to be enjoyed again and again."

"These sermons, articles, and book reviews, collected from Warfield's writings, show the genuine stamp of Reformed experiential piety that rested on the great 19th-century Princeton theologians. The sermons on the leading and sealing of the Spirit are themselves worth the price of the book. Would you like guidance in learning how to live more closely to Christ, how to walk more by faith through the Spirit, and how to wrestle at the throne of grace? Read this book prayerfully, both for clarity of mind and warmth of soul with regard to the person and ministry of the blessed Spirit. Let Warfield be your spiritual mentor in the great things of God." - Joel Beeke

***THE OFFICE AND WORK OF THE HOLY SPIRIT*** by James Buchanan
"James Buchanan belonged to the bright galaxy of theologians who graced the early days of the Free Church of Scotland. His brilliant and uniquely conceived treatment of the Holy Spirit expounds his Ministry first biblically and theologically, then in a series of biographical studies, and finally systematically in the life of the Christian. Buchanan superbly combines the reliable with the readable, the doctrinal with the practical, the theological with the devotional. 'The Office and Work of the Holy Spirit' is a classic work on the Holy Spirit and a master class in theology." - Sinclair Ferguson

**SOLID GROUND CHRISTIAN BOOKS**
**1682 Pancoast St., Port St Lucie FL 34987**
www.solid-ground-books.com
mike.sgcb@gmail.com
**205-587-4480**

www.ingramcontent.com/pod-product-compliance
Lightning Source LLC
Chambersburg PA
CBHW070323100426
42743CB00011B/2530